*Portugal and the Quest
for the Indies*

Part of a map of the world by Henry Martellus (c. 1490)

CHRISTOPHER BELL

Portugal and the Quest for the Indies

BARNES & NOBLE
BOOKS
10 East 53d St., New York 10022
(a division of Harper & Row Publishers, Inc.)

Published in the U.S.A. 1974 by
Harper & Row Publishers, Inc.
Barnes & Noble Import Division

ISBN - 06-490352-4

Contents

Illustrations

Illustrations

To my Wife

THE HOUSE OF AVIS

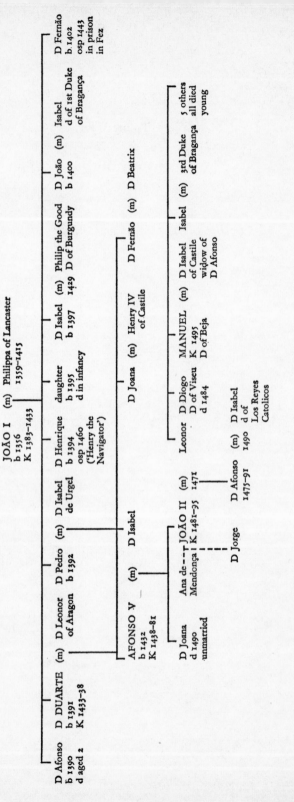

THE HOUSE OF BRAGANÇA

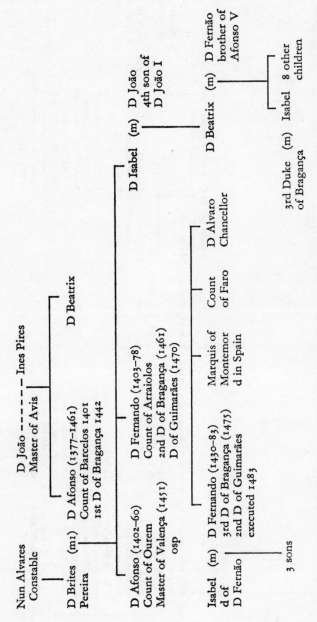

The titles and estates, which the third Duke had forfeited in 1483, were restored by MANUEL after his accession. The Bragança kings, who ruled Portugal from 1640 onwards, were direct descendants, as was Catherine of Bragança who married Charles II of England.

RELATIONSHIPS OF JOÃO I WITH THE ROYAL HOUSES
OF PORTUGAL, ENGLAND AND CASTILE

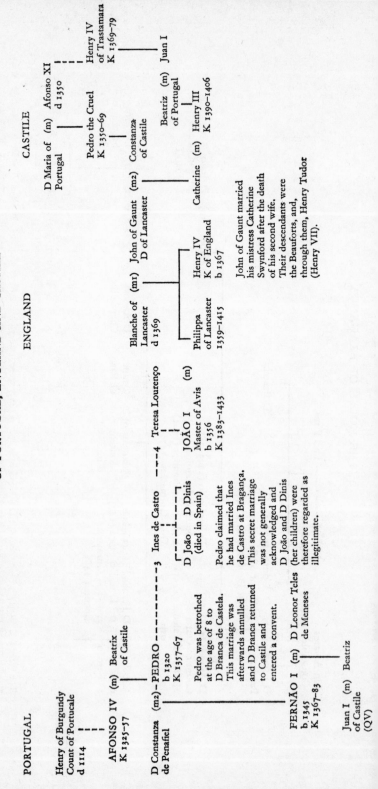

FIFTEENTH-CENTURY SOVEREIGNS OF CASTILE

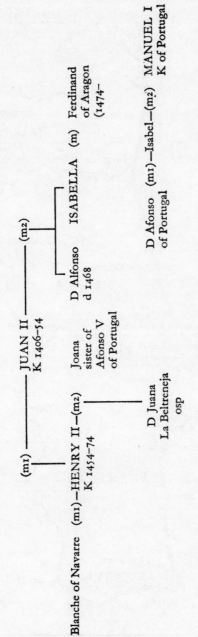

PORTUGAL

MINHO

Bragança

Guimarães

TRAS OS
MONTES

Portó

Douro

S
P
A
I
N

Vizeu

Mondego

Guarda

Coimbra

BEIRA

Leiria

Batalha

Alcobaça · ✗ Aljubarrota

Tagus

R I B A T E J O

Santarém

✗ Alfarrobeira

LISBON ·

Elvas

Evora

A L E N T E J O

Sines

Monchique

A L G A R V E

Cape St
Vincent

Lagos

Sagres

The Master of Avis

On the 14th February 1387, Philippa of Lancaster, daughter of John of Gaunt, was married at Oporto to King João I of Portugal. The Portuguese chronicler, Fernão Lopes, has left us a description of the wedding.

'With her bridegroom at her side, the Lady Philippa rode through the streets of the town from the Bishop's Palace, where she had been staying, to the Cathedral. Mounted on a white horse, she was clad in cloth of gold, a golden crown set with precious stones on her head, and on her breast the gold brooch, worked with pearls and other gems, which the King had given her at the ceremony of their betrothal twelve days before.

'The Archbishop of Braga held her bridle. A band of pipers and trumpeters led the way. Great nobles followed on horseback and behind them well-born ladies and the wives and daughters of the citizens came singing, as was the custom at such festivities. The streets were swept and garnished, decorated with all manner of green branches and sweet smelling herbs. But as the way was short, the crowd was so great that it could not easily be confined and kept in order.

'At the door of the Church, Dom Roderigo, Bishop of Oporto, in his festival robes, met the bridal couple. He took them by the hand and pronounced over them the words which the Holy Church orders to be used at this sacrament. And after he had said Mass and preached, the

King and Queen returned to the Palace from which they had set out. There tables laden with food had been prepared, not only for the bride and groom, who sat apart, but for the nobles and the burgesses of the city. In charge of this occasion was Nun' Álvares Pereira, the Constable of Portugal: the servers were lords and knights, *fidalgos* of the realm, and the Englishmen, John Holland, Philippa's brother-in-law, Thomas Percy and Richard Burley, whom the Queen had brought with her.

'Musicians, jugglers and tumblers entertained the guests in the great hall while they were feasting, and when the banquet was finished, they all rose up and began to dance and some of the ladies to sing, which gave great pleasure to the company. The King went meanwhile to his room, and in the evening after supper, the Archbishop and other prelates blessed the royal bed with the prayers appointed for such a time. At last the King and Queen retired, and the guests, bishops and nobles, knights and burgesses, and their ladies, went home to their lodgings[1].'

John of Gaunt was not present at his daughter's wedding, nor was Philippa's stepmother, Dona Constanza. They were, says Lopes, 'wholly engaged with their forthcoming attack on the Kingdom of Castile'.

João I, Master of Avis, was destined to be the founder of a royal line which was to occupy the throne of Portugal throughout the most important two hundred years of her history. His descendants were to preside over the astonishing series of adventures which form the subject of this book; over the brief years of glory when the ascendancy of the Portuguese in the East was almost undisputed, and over the rapid erosion of her influence as her moral and physical reserves became exhausted. The last of them, the young King Sebastian, was killed in battle against the Moors in 1578: two years later, the crowns of Spain and Portugal were united under Philip II and for sixty years Portugal ceased to exist as an independent country.

At the time of his marriage in 1387, however, D. João's hold on his throne was still precarious and the danger from his Castilian neighbour very real. Besides Portugal, there were at this time four kingdoms in the Iberian peninsula: in the north, the mountain state of Navarre straddled the Pyrenees; in the east, the princes of Aragon ruled not only in Aragon itself, but in Catalonia, Valencia and the Balearic Islands, which they had recently added to their dominions; in the south, the Sultans of Granada still firmly held the region of inaccessible mountains and fertile valleys which was all that remained of the conquests the Islamic invaders had made when they poured out of Africa six hundred years before. The whole of central Spain, together with Galicia in the north-west, made up the Kingdom of Castile and Leon, ruled over by Juan I of the house of Trastamara.

Although the tide of the Muslim invasions in the eighth century had quickly reached its peak and begun at once slowly to ebb, it was four hundred years before Portugal began to emerge from the welter of quarrelsome Christian states in northern Spain. The foundations were laid by an eleventh-century adventurer, Henry, a son of the Duke of Burgundy. Created Count of Portucale, he did his best to carve himself a principality from the lands between the Minho and Douro rivers which had been won from the Moors and entrusted to his care by Afonso VI of Leon. But it was only towards the end of the long life of the Count's son, Afonso Henriques, who succeeded him as a small boy in 1114 and lived until 1185, that the title of King of Portugal was recognized both by his former overlord and by the Pope. Meanwhile, from his birthplace and capital at Guimarães, Afonso Henriques had pushed the Muslims further and further south. In 1147, with the help of some crusaders on their way to the Holy Land, he captured Lisbon. But the fighting swayed to and fro and it was not until a century later that the Muslim strongholds in the south were finally reduced and the frontiers of Portugal established much as they are today.

The train of events which led to the eclipse of the House of Burgundy and to John of Gaunt's Spanish adventures may be said to have begun about 1350 during the reign of Pedro the Cruel of Castile. Whether this monarch fully deserved his reputation or not, he certainly stirred up for himself formidable opposition by his relentless treatment of those of the Castilian nobility whose loyalty was in doubt and by the suspicion that he had caused the death by poisoning of his French Queen, Blanche of Bourbon.

His enemies were divided among themselves. There were those who supported his illegitimate half-brother, Henry of Trastamara, and those who favoured another Pedro, the heir of King Afonso IV of Portugal. The idea of the union, or rather the re-union, of Castile and Portugal was to be an ever-recurring theme, but in this case the leaders of the faction were the brothers of Ines de Castro, the Galician beauty with whom the Portuguese prince had fallen deeply in love. The story of Pedro and Ines, who lie buried in splendid tombs in the great monastery church of Alcobaça, is one of the classics of Portuguese history, but lies beyond the scope of this book. It had an abrupt and unhappy ending. In 1355, rather than risk a war with Castile, King Afonso ordered his son's mistress to be put to death. The danger to Castile from Portugal thus died away, but as far as Portugal itself was concerned, this was not yet the end of the matter. For in later years Pedro claimed that he had been secretly married to Ines in the remote northern town of Bragança, and the claims of their children to the throne of Portugal had afterwards to be taken into account.

In Castile, Pedro the Cruel faced a much more serious threat, for his rival, Henry of Trastamara, had the support of France. It was not the domestic quarrels of the Castilians which interested the French, but the powerful fleet which their King could put at the disposal of his allies. Pedro had entered into an alliance with England, and so involved himself and his country in the Hundred Years War.

With the help of the French, Henry of Trastamara was soon able to drive Pedro out, only to be defeated in his turn at Najera by the Black Prince, who in 1367, tardily and at a price, had arrived from his base in Gascony to the help of his deposed ally. The results of this victory were, however, short-lived; two years later, again with French assistance, Henry gained the upper hand once more: Pedro was forced to surrender and was forthwith murdered in Henry's presence.

In 1371 John of Gaunt made himself leader of the legitimist party of Castile by marrying Dona Constanza, elder surviving daughter of Pedro the Cruel: his first wife, Blanche of Lancaster, the mother of Philippa and of the future Henry IV of England, had died in the previous year. He now assumed the titles of King of Castile and Leon, Duke of Lancaster, but it was to be fifteen years before he could make a serious attempt to make good his claim. In England, the demands on men and money for the war with France always came first and neither the Commons nor the King's advisers felt inclined to support a venture which seemed to have no object beyond the personal aggrandizement of the Duke of Lancaster.

It was the activities of the Castilian fleet which made them change their minds. As has been seen, the royal galleys of Castile were regarded by the French as an important pawn on the political board, for they were a formidable force in conditions which suited them. In the fourteenth century it was no disgrace to serve in them, even at the oars. Though they had their limitations, especially in bad weather, they were fast, and, being at the direct disposal of the King, readily available. In England, by contrast, the Government had to rely, both for ships of war and transports, on the cumbersome and unpopular process of 'arrest'.

From 1377 onwards French and Spanish raiders, carried in Castilian galleys, descended on the south coast towns of England from Cornwall to Kent, burning and destroying them, and even on one occasion marching inland to sack the Priory at Lewes.

Such indignities naturally made the English Government reconsider its policy in the Peninsula. The obvious ally was now Portugal, not only because of the growing importance of Anglo-Portuguese trade since the loss of the markets in Castile, but also because it was easy to reach and lay close to the heart of Castilian territory. As it happened, King Fernão was very willing to listen to advances from England. During the ten-year reign of his father – that same Pedro who as a young man had become entangled with Castilian affairs through Ines de Castro – the Portuguese had stood aside from the disturbances over the border. But Fernão, who succeeded to the throne in 1367, young, romantic and impulsive, had thrown himself enthusiastically into the fray on the side of the legitimists, and by doing so had plunged his country into near disaster. He had also alienated many of his own people, especially the Lisboetas, by his marriage to Leonor Teles de Meneses. Not only was Leonor already married to somebody else, so that Fernão had to obtain a Papal dispensation in order to marry her himself, but her reputation was by no means unblemished.

In due course the slow-moving wheels of English recruiting procedure produced a small army for Portugal, and in 1381 Fernão embarked on a new campaign against Castile. He now had to face Juan I, for the swashbuckling Henry of Trastamara was dead. The campaign eventually ground to a halt: the English contingent, under the miserable Earl of Cambridge, hampered by the indecision of its leaders, by sickness and even by a mutiny, was of very little use; by the peace which was signed when both sides were exhausted, Fernão's nine-year-old daughter Beatriz was betrothed to Juan of Castile.

King Fernão now fell seriously ill and it was left to Juan Fernández de Andeiro, Count of Ourem, to work out the details of the marriage settlement. It was an odd choice: Andeiro was a Castilian, a supporter of the legitimist cause and Lancaster's representative in Portugal: he was also the lover of Queen Leonor whose unpopularity he shared. The agreement he signed was a complicated document. Among other things, it provided that if King Fernão died without a male heir, D. Beatriz would be Queen of Portugal; if D. Beatriz had a son he would be King of Portugal; but if Fernão died before Beatriz had a son or before she reached the age of fourteen, the Regency would be entrusted to Queen Leonor.

In the event Juan and Beatriz had been married only five months, when, in October 1383, King Fernão died. Before his death he had neither the opportunity, nor perhaps the will, to modify the settlement; the conduct of affairs, therefore, passed to Leonor who assumed the title of Regent. Though Andeiro and his supporters defended the arrangements he had made as a genuine attempt to cover all possible contingencies and to ensure a peaceful succession when Fernão died, they had failed to take sufficiently into account the intense unpopularity of Leonor Teles and the ambitions of Juan of Castile. The citizens of Lisbon and Oporto regarded the agreement as a betrayal of their national interests: Juan saw a chance in the turn events had taken of gaining immediate possession of Portugal. Against the advice of his councillors he at once crossed the Portuguese frontier and occupied Guarda: most of the leading *fidalgos*, bound more by their oaths of fealty to the royal family than by patriotic sentiment, took his part and delivered the border towns and fortresses for which they were responsible into his hands.

Meanwhile the Lisboetas, faced with this threat to their independence, and more hostile than ever to the Queen-Regent and her lover, called on D. João, Master of Avis, to save them from Leonor Teles and the Castilians. Amid scenes of great excitement, D. João broke into the Palace at the head of a body of armed men, assassinated Andeiro in the Queen's presence, and was acclaimed 'Regent and Defender of the Kingdom' by the people of Lisbon. Leonor Teles fled to Santarém, where she resigned her office to Juan of Castile.

The future King João I was the illegitimate son of D. Pedro, who, after the death of Ines de Castro, had consoled himself with a lady named Teresa Lourenço. D. João was twenty-six at the time of the death of his half-brother King Fernão by whom he had been created Master of the military order of Avis. There seems no reason to suppose that at first he had designs on the throne for

himself, and indeed, his first actions were taken in the
name of the Infante D. João, elder son of D. Pedro and
Ines de Castro, who with his brother D. Denis, was in
exile in Castile. But the situation in which the new Regent
found himself was anything but promising: at Santarém
the King of Castile was almost on his doorstep; many
important towns and most of northern Portugal had
declared for his enemies; his opponents included not only
the supporters of Juan and Leonor Teles, but even some
of those who favoured the claims of the Infante D. João.
He had no possible ally except England and the evidence
of the campaign of 1381–2 did not suggest that aid from
that quarter would be very valuable.

Against all this he had the backing of the merchants of
Lisbon and Oporto who were able to save him from
financial worries; of the professional classes, especially the
lawyers, who were ready to give him advice; of the Lisbon
mob, which was vociferous but ineffectual, and of a soldier
of outstanding ability in Nun' Álvares Pereira, who was
one of the few men of noble birth to take his side, and
who, as Constable of Portugal, was to make a conspicuous
contribution to the survival of the new régime.

Despite all expectations to the contrary, D. João's
position at the end of 1384 was somewhat stronger than
it had been a year earlier. King Juan of Castile had put
the two young Infantes in prison and thus made his own
intentions crystal clear: at the beginning of the summer
he had laid siege to Lisbon but had been forced to withdraw
at the end of it with the loss, through plague and famine,
of a large part of his army and most of his experienced
commanders. A number of important men, including
Fogaça, the Chancellor of the dead King Fernão, had
deserted him: between them D. João and Nun' Álvares
had recovered a number of towns and castles, while at

Os Atoleiros in Alentejo, the Constable, making use of the same kind of defensive tactics which had served English armies so well against heavily armoured French knights, had routed a Castilian force much more numerous than his own.

Soon the supporters of D. João felt strong enough to take a further step forward. Early in April 1385 the Cortes met at Coimbra to resolve the question of the succession. Since its members were determined at all costs to preserve the independence of their country, the claims of D. Beatriz, who was certainly the legal heir, were rejected. Her husband, as King of Castile, was unacceptable. There were, however, still many supporters of the Infante D. João, but they were finally silenced by the lawyer, Dr. João das Regras. While the decision hung in the balance, he produced documents which showed, he said, that D. Pedro and Ines de Castro were related; that because of this D. Pedro had appealed to the Pope for a dispensation to allow him to marry Ines, and that this dispensation the Pope had refused. Their children were therefore no more legitimate than the Master of Avis himself. In these circumstances, he declared, the Cortes could elect whom it liked. The Cortes did. On 6th April the crown was formally offered to D. João and he was proclaimed King of Portugal.

Meanwhile a few hundred English archers and men-at-arms, recruited by the envoys D. João had sent to the court of Richard II, had arrived in Lisbon, a small but useful addition to the new King's strength. He would need all the help he could get, for Juan of Castile had been busying himself with collecting a fresh and yet more formidable army and was preparing to invade Portugal once more.

The first part of the campaign of 1385, however, went in favour of D. João. He and the Constable were able to recover more towns and castles, and a strong Castilian raiding party, laden with the spoils of the monasteries and churches at Viseu, was soundly thrashed at Trancoso. Nevertheless, by the beginning of August, Juan was once more well on his way to Lisbon and his fleet was already in the Tagus blockading the city from the sea.

King João and the Constable decided to fight, but on ground of their own choosing. On 14th August they took up their position across the road from Coimbra to Lisbon, a few miles south of Leiria and north of the village of Aljubarrota, which was to give the coming battle its name. It was a strong defensive position, on a spur between the steep valleys of two streams, so strong that when the Castilian vanguard finally reached it late in the morning, they decided not to risk a frontal attack, but embarked instead on a long and laborious cross-country march to outflank it. Towards evening they emerged once more on the main road to the south.

During the afternoon the Portuguese had plenty of time to reverse their order of battle, while the King, Nun' Álvares and the Archbishop of Braga encouraged them in the names of the Blessed Virgin and St. George. They were in good heart, for although they now had open ground in front of them, their flanks were still guarded by the same two valleys. Juan now had to decide what to do next, whether to continue his march to Lisbon, or to give his men, who were hot, thirsty and tired, a night's rest, or to attack at once. He himself might well have preferred to wait, but about six o'clock matters were taken out of his hands; some of his young firebrands, confident of victory and eager for glory, gave the signal to advance.

The battle now took a course which was to be repeated thirty years later at Agincourt. The Castilians, though much more numerous and heavily armed than their opponents, committed themselves piecemeal in a disorderly throng, on a front which was much too narrow for them to make use of their superior numbers or even to wield their weapons in comfort. They failed to break the Portuguese centre at the first impact and soon found themselves in trouble from the archers stationed on the flanks, among them the English contingent. The fight was short but bloody before the Castilians broke: when darkness fell, Juan had abandoned his army and was on his way to join his garrison at Santarém: he had lost more than two thousand men.

Below the hill where the Portuguese had first taken up their position on this eventful day now stands the great abbey church of Batalha which King João built to celebrate his victory and to fulfil a vow he had made on the morning of the battle.

The defeat of the Castilians at Aljubarrota greatly strengthened D. João's hold on his kingdom, especially as many of the Portuguese notables who had supported his rival were among the dead. But even now he could not ignore his long, vulnerable frontier, and with this in mind he set about encouraging John of Gaunt to make good his neglected claim to the throne of Castile. His representations to England were now well received, not only because of the constant threat to the south coast towns from Castilian galleys in alliance with the French, but also because at this time Richard II was only too pleased to see his powerful uncle gainfully employed in a foreign land. In return for the assistance of a squadron of Portuguese galleys in the Channel, the Government of England undertook to supply an army under the command of John of Gaunt for the invasion of Castile.

Inevitably it took time to assemble the troops and the ships to carry them, so that it was the end of July 1386

before Lancaster finally disembarked at Corunna. To begin
with, his operations in Galicia were very successful, for
there he could still count on many of the supporters of
his dead father-in-law. Unfortunately the season for
campaigning was already nearing its end and he soon had
to set up his headquarters in Orense for the winter. The
next few months were largely spent in negotiations with
the King of Portugal, until at Ponte de Mouro D. João
agreed to keep an army in being against the Castilians until
the following autumn, in return for the hand of Philippa
of Lancaster in marriage and the cession of a strip
of Castilian territory adjoining the eastern frontier of
Portugal.

After all this, the events which followed were something
of an anticlimax. By the spring Lancaster's force had been
much reduced by sickness and the King of Castile had
been given time to prepare himself and to send for rein-
forcements from France. For some weeks the Duke and
his Portuguese allies marched and counter-marched through
the countryside of western Castile without capturing any
major fortress or indeed achieving anything much of
importance. The English and Gascon knights were inclined
to spend their time in tourneys and other chivalrous
exercises with their French opposite numbers in the
Castilian camp, much to the annoyance of the Portuguese
to whom this war was a serious business. Eventually it
turned out that Lancaster and King Juan had for some
time been in touch with each other and were preparing
to sign an agreement by which Lancaster was to give up
his personal claim to the thrones of Castile and Leon and
Juan was to bring the dynastic feud to an end by marrying
Catalina, the Duke's youngest daughter: her mother was
Dona Constanza and she was the grand-daughter, therefore,
of Pedro the Cruel.

The English army then melted away and John of Gaunt went home. He had conveniently forgotten his previous agreement with D. João and had failed even to ensure that his new son-in-law would recognize the independence of Portugal.

The Enterprise of Ceuta

Queen Philippa and her husband had little in common, but they made a good team. The court historian, Fernão Lopes, said of D. João: 'His speech was always thoughtful and courteous; no insults nor bad language ever passed his lips, nor was he ever ill-tempered or arrogant. Even his reproaches were bland and restrained, so that both the virtues required of a king–justice and piety–were combined in his person.'

A portrait, said to be contemporary, shows him in an attitude of prayer. It suggests a man serious and determined, who would think well before he took action and keep his thoughts to himself. He was short and dark, favouring his mother perhaps, for the Burgundian kings are said to have been tall and fair; by no means guileless, for his small, rather protruding eyes seem to look sidelong at his visitors. He was by nature cautious and self-controlled, and the atmosphere of intrigue in which he grew up would have encouraged him to feel his way before committing himself. He would also have learnt, and must quickly unlearn now that he was married, that in the inbred courts of the peninsula, extra-marital affairs and illegitimacy were a commonplace. He himself was a bastard; his sister-in-law Leonor Teles had taken Count Andeiro as her lover; his great friend and ally, the Constable Nun' Álvares, was the son of a Prior of Crato and the grandson of an Archbishop of Braga, both of whom had taken vows of chastity;

his own bastard son, Afonso, was to marry the daughter of Nun' Álvares and found the House of Bragança.

In spite of his royal blood, D. João had the common touch. The *arraia-miuda*, the humble folk, supported him to a man: what was more important, the merchants, burgesses and professional men were also on his side, and from them he drew most of the executive officers of his government.

But Queen Philippa was an aristocrat to her finger-tips: she was also very English. She was tall, blonde and trim; not beautiful, but with good features and a fresh complexion. She was strong-minded, strait-laced and managing— even bossy. In many respects she took after her mother, Blanche of Lancaster. Fernão Lopes says of her, 'Her conversation was sincere and of benefit to many: she was without pride in her royal estate and spoke sweetly and pleasantly to all. She often gave great pleasure by joining in the games her damsels played. She would pass over genuine mistakes, and was friendly to all honest persons[2].'

Certainly her influence on the Portuguese Court was profound. So, too, through her children, was her influence on the course of Portuguese history. She was praised by her contemporaries for putting her duty as queen, wife and mother before her own wishes, but a court historian could not be expected to add that she was determined to get her own way and not at all sympathetic to human weaknesses. She stamped ruthlessly on immorality at the Court and among the nobility, which previously had been taken for granted. Her husband, who saw clearly where his best interests lay, turned himself into a model husband and father.

Her children were devoted to their father, to herself and to Portugal. Camões calls them *a ínclita geração*[3], the noble generation, and it is with their story that the next five chapters are largely concerned. Two children, the eldest son and a girl, died in infancy, but the six who survived had more than ordinary attainments which their mother did much to encourage and develop. The heir to the throne was D. Duarte (Edward), who took his name from his Plantagenet ancestors: studious and meticulous, upright and a lover of justice, he was unfortunately more of a theorist than a man of action and probably less well fitted to be a king than any of the others. Since his father lived to be seventy-five, he succeeded to the throne only in middle age and his five-year reign is remembered chiefly for the disaster at Tangier. His brother, D. Pedro, philosopher, traveller and economist, yet shrewd and practical, had, as will be seen, much more influence on the course of events than has usually been attributed to him. His ideas were often much ahead of his time, but in the end he was to fall a victim to the reactionary forces of the age in which he lived. The third son, D. Henrique, known to us as Henry the Navigator, won and has retained a reputation possibly greater than he deserved. Although every word he wrote and every recorded action has been subjected to the most minute scrutiny, his personality and his motives still remain something of a mystery.

The three younger children have received less attention. D. Isabel, the only girl, married Philip the Good of Burgundy, and did much to help him make his Court a centre of art and learning. The few references to D. João suggest that he resembled Pedro, but, plagued by ill-health and overshadowed by his three elder brothers, he made no great name for himself. D. Fernão, the youngest, born when the Queen was forty-two, fell into the hands of the Moors at the siege of Tangier and died in prison at Fez. Romantic and deeply religious, he bore his sufferings bravely. After his death he was to be hailed as a martyr and remembered as the 'Saintly Prince'.

Although the Kings of Portugal and Castile were married to step-sisters whose influence was on the side of peace, a state of war continued to exist between the two countries for many years. But as the Castilian nobility had suffered so severely at the siege of Lisbon and at Aljubarrota, the fighting was confined to border skirmishes and there were long periods of truce. D. João was determined that any treaty of peace should include recognition of his country's independence and this for a long time D. Juan and his successors were unwilling to grant. At last, however, in 1411 the war came officially to an end and D. João was able to turn his attention to other matters.

Among other things he had to consider the future of his three elder sons; like most young nobles of their time they were eager to prove their manhood by distinguishing themselves in battle. It seems to have been their father's intention to organize for them an international tourney, to celebrate the end of the war with Castile and to show that Portugal was worthy of a place among the nations of Europe. Besides banquets and other entertainments, his sons would joust with suitable opponents and be duly rewarded with the accolade of knighthood. But such an artificial kind of warfare was not at all to the liking of the young princes who set about looking for a more genuine substitute.

They found it in a proposal to attack the Moorish port of Ceuta which lay across the straits on the north coast of Africa opposite Gibraltar. The 'Enterprise of Ceuta', as it came to be called, was not their own idea but it appealed strongly to the religious convictions they had inherited

English archers arriving at Lisbon before the battle of Aljubarrota, 1385

English archers at the battle of Aljubarrota, 1385

from their mother. The King had been turning the project over in his mind for some time, ever since it had first been suggested to him by João Afonso, the Treasurer of his Household. He saw that it had its attractions, for it was to appeal both to the nobility and to the burgesses who still formed the backbone of his government.

For the nobility anything which promised excitement and loot was better than the daily round on their estates. Since so much of the business of the kingdom was now in the hands of their social inferiors many of them were very much under-employed; like the young princes they longed to gain glory in battle, and to emulate their elders whose recollections of the campaigns they had fought in their youth had, no doubt, lost nothing in the telling. Although he lived in complete retirement, Nun' Álvares was still the hero of Portugal. War in the service of God and the King was still the trade of a respectable medieval knight and a war against their ancient enemies, the Moors, could not fail to gain them credit in the sight of God. In addition, they might expect 'honours and mercies' from the King as a reward for their exploits, titles and grants of money and land. For they still depended almost entirely on their estates to support themselves and their retainers and, since the coming of the Black Death in the middle of the previous century, revenues from land had dropped steeply. The King himself, of course, also relied largely on his estates for his own and the national income and he, since he had already made extensive grants to his supporters, could not afford to give away more. A successful campaign in North Africa might solve this problem for him.

Neither the prospect of a new Crusade nor the lure of titles and land greatly interested the hard-headed merchants of the towns. They were tempted by hope of improved trade. Portuguese ships carrying fish and salt, olive oil, wine and cork, had long been a familiar sight in ports as far away as Flanders and England, and the Treaty of Windsor, which made Portugal England's 'oldest ally' had been signed in 1394. But the merchants of Oporto and Lisbon cast jealous eyes on the rich carrying trade of the Mediterranean and the two great republics of Venice and Genoa which supplied Europe with almost all the luxuries they then knew. The sources of all this wealth were in Muslim hands and Ceuta, one of the most westerly ports of the Arab world, shared in the profits of this trade.

There was more to it than this. Ceuta was a terminus of the trans-Saharan trade, a staging post through which some of the gold of Guinea trickled into Europe. The town overlooked the Straits, the gateway to the Mediterranean, and as such had already attracted the attention of Castile, and even of Genoa. It could not be allowed to fall into rival hands. It could afford shelter for Christian ships running from the corsairs of the Barbary coast; at the same time it could provide a base from which Portuguese ships could prey on Arab merchantmen. There were rich fisheries which the Portuguese could use off the Atlantic coast of North Africa: the weavers of the Kingdom of Fez made cloth which was exported through Ceuta and which sold well in southern Europe. Finally, the hinterland of Ceuta was at that time a rich agricultural area which not only carried large herds of cattle, sheep and goats, but which also produced substantial quantities of wheat – often scarce in the Iberian peninsula.

It seemed to the merchants and to men like João Afonso and João das Regras that if they could lay their hands on Ceuta they would acquire a rich prize of permanent worth, but they now had to persuade the King that the Enterprise would be both possible and profitable. For this, according to the chroniclers, they relied on the youthful enthusiasm of D. Henrique and his two elder brothers, who in turn enlisted the help of their mother and their half-brother, Afonso, Count of Arraiolos. They set themselves to out-argue their father.

D. João was already over fifty years old. He may well have hoped to end his days in peace and quiet. In any case, however glamorous or profitable a new war might seem to others, he was not going to be jumped into a hasty decision, even by his sons. 'Even supposing', he said, 'that an expedition against the Moors would bring credit to the realm, might it not be better to attack the Kingdom of Granada? True, this would offend Castile, but the city could be reached by land without the need for ships and their crews, nor the money to pay for them, none of which could easily be found.'

'Why not', suggested D. Henrique, 'ask the merchants for a loan? Since they would gain so much from the Enterprise, they should surely invest money in it. Then we could hire ships and their crews to carry the army across the Straits. As to soldiers, now that the war with Castile is won, there will certainly be no lack of volunteers.'

D. João allowed himself to be persuaded; he must, however, he told them, consult both his Council and Nun' Álvares. The Council supported the project, for most of them were in the secret already. The Constable, perhaps rather to the King's surprise, was equally enthusiastic. 'It appears to me', he said, 'that this plan was not conceived by you, nor by anyone in this world, but was inspired by God.'

With this blessing the Enterprise could go forward. Every effort had to be made to ensure its success and so it was decided that the destination of the expedition should remain a secret. Although a hundred or more people, the King and his family, the Council, the merchants who contributed to the loan, knew all about it; although the shipyards of the Tagus and the Douro hummed with activity; although the beaches were piled high with the stores of chandlers and victuallers; although D. Pedro, D. Henrique and D. Afonso were scouring the countryside for recruits, and in every village weapons and armour were being fashioned or refurbished, a secret it apparently remained until the morning of 13th August 1415 when the fleet dropped anchor under the walls of Ceuta.

While these preparations were going on D. João devoted all his ingenuity to concealing his real intentions. First he sent his Chancellor, Fernão Fogaça, to threaten the Duke of Holland with war if he did not restrain those of his subjects who cheated and robbed Portuguese merchants trading in his country. He told Fogaça to seek a private interview with the Duke and to tell him that the threat was a pretence, but to ask him to accept the challenge as if it were genuine, so that the Moors might not be alarmed by the warlike preparations in Portugal.

D. João also sent an embassy to the Queen of Sicily to offer her one of his younger sons in marriage. But since he well knew that the Queen would only be interested in marrying his heir, this was naturally a fruitless expedition. But the two ambassadors, Afonso Furtado de Mendonça, and the Prior of the Hospital, Álvaro Gonçalves, were given secret instructions to make an excuse to visit Ceuta on the way back and to take a close look at its fortifications.

The King and his sons impatiently awaited the return of the ambassadors at the Palace at Cintra. At first they had to restrain their impatience: Afonso Furtado began with a long rigmarole about how, many years ago, when he had visited Ceuta with his father, he had watered his horse at a well, and how an old Moor had told him that he had seen in a vision the King of Portugal watering his horse at this same well. This, he said, was a sure sign that the attack would be successful. When his turn came, Álvaro Gonçalves asked for two sacks of sand, a roll of ribbon, half a bushel of beans and a small basin. The King, who wanted not prophecies nor astrology but facts, began to grow irritable, but when Gonçalves insisted, he gave him what he asked and waited while the ambassador shut himself into a small room. At last Gonçalves called them in, to show them a detailed relief map he had prepared. The sand and the basin were the land and hills round Ceuta, the beans were the houses and the ribbon the walls of the city. The strengths and weaknesses of their objective were clearly exposed.

By the early summer of 1415 the preparations were almost complete and worried ambassadors from Castile, Granada and elsewhere came hurrying to Portugal hoping for reassurances that all this activity was not directed against their countries. On 10th July D. Henrique's squadron of seventy ships from Oporto appeared in the Tagus, with trumpets blowing and banners emblazoned with their leader's device, *talent de bien faire*. They were greeted enthusiastically by the people of Lisbon crowding the water's edge at Restelo below the city.

The Lisboetas had need of something to hearten them, for their unwelcome summer visitor, the plague, was once more raging. D. Pedro, who had come to the city to meet his brother, had to tell him that the Queen was among the sick and that she lay dangerously ill at Odivelas. The two princes set out at once on horseback to join D. Duarte at their mother's bedside. It was clear that Queen Philippa was dying, but when they arrived she summoned her remaining strength and called for the three swords she had had especially made for the expedition to Ceuta.

One by one she addressed her sons: to D. Duarte she said,

'My son, God has chosen you among your brothers that you may be heir to this kingdom, and that you may hold in your hands its Government and its justice. Knowing your virtue and your kindness, I give you this sword of justice, with which you may govern both great and small, when, at the death of your father, this realm shall be yours. I pray you always be watchful that right and justice be served. And, note well, my son, that when I say justice, I mean justice with compassion, for justice without mercy is not to be called justice, but cruelty. I have caused this sword to be made and with it the other two, and I had wished that all you three might be made knights by your father in my presence before your departure. But God has willed it otherwise.'

To Pedro she said, 'My son, since your childhood I have seen how greatly you respect the service of ladies and damsels, which is one of the things which is to be especially commended in a knight. I have reminded your brother of his duty to his people. I now recommend you always to have in mind the defence of the ladies and the protection of their honour and happiness.'

And lastly to D. Henrique she said, 'This third sword I have kept for you. As you are strong, so it is strong. I have charged one of your brothers to protect the people and the other the ladies. To you I wish to commend all the nobility, knights and esquires of this realm, for albeit they all belong to the King and he is careful of all of them according to their condition, yet they may often have need of your aid to maintain their rights and receive the benefits they deserve . . . I give you this sword with my blessing, and I desire that with it you should receive the accolade of knighthood.'

Henry answered, 'Lady, be sure that as long as my life lasts I will keep in my heart the memory of your commands and I will employ all my power and all my goodwill to obey you.'

Queen Philippa lay back exhausted, but still her mind stayed clear. Before she died, she roused herself to hear the muttering of the wind outside the Palace. 'What wind is blowing?' she asked. 'The north wind', they told her. 'That will be the best for your voyage', whispered the dying woman, 'I had hoped to assist . . .'

With the Queen's death it seemed that the Enterprise might be abandoned. The King was overcome with grief and could not make up his mind: the people of Lisbon, many of whom had lost kinsmen in the plague, were further saddened by this national loss: an eclipse of the sun, which spread gloom over the city, was taken as an omen of disaster. Only D. Henrique kept his grip on realities; although he felt his mother's death as much as did his father or his brothers, he sent a message to the King, pointing out that the fleet and the army could not be kept together for long: if they were once dispersed, they could not be gathered again: the secret of their destination could not indefinitely be kept: it was, he reminded his father, his mother's dying wish that the Enterprise should go forward.

D. João acquiesced, and on 23rd July, only five days after the death of the Queen, the expedition set sail. At first all went well: the favourable north wind carried them quickly beyond Cape St. Vincent. But then things began to go wrong: they were becalmed for a week off Lagos and, when they did reach Ceuta, high winds blew them back to Europe again before they could do more than put ashore a small party of men and fight an insignificant skirmish. While they waited for the storm to subside the more faint-hearted were for returning home. D. João again suggested that they should attack Granada instead. This time it was the Constable who persuaded the King to return to Ceuta.

In the event the town fell to the Portuguese in a single day, with the loss, so the chroniclers tell us, of only eight lives. Fortunately Sala-bin-Sala, King of Fez and overlord of Ceuta, thought that his enemies had given up the assault and had made no attempt to strengthen the garrison. The Portuguese, landing from small boats on open beaches, were determined and courageous. D. Henrique led the way into the town with a small band of followers and plunged recklessly into the maze of narrow streets where a resolute enemy could so easily have ambushed him and cut his men to pieces. At Ceuta, as at Tangier, more than twenty years later, this usually cautious and deliberate prince lost his head in the excitement of battle. This time he was lucky: resistance was feeble and soon the whole town was in Portuguese hands. After nightfall, even the citadel was given up without a fight.

As was the custom, Ceuta was put to the sack on the night of its capture and, as was also the custom, those who had distinguished themselves in battle were rewarded. The mosque was consecrated immediately for Christian rights: a thanksgiving mass was celebrated in a mood of pious jubilation, and the three young princes received the accolade of knighthood from their father with the swords their mother had given them.

On 2nd September the Portuguese fleet sailed for home to be received there with high enthusiasm. While Portugal rejoiced, the King's nephew, Henry V of England, was setting out on the long march through northern France which was to lead him to victory at Agincourt.

The Portuguese had their prize but its immediate benefits were hard to see. The palaces and warehouses of the Arab merchants had been plundered by uncouth peasants from the mountain villages of Tras-os-Montes and Beira in a feverish search for gold and silver. Ebony chests full of silks from the East, priceless furnishings and oriental carpets, valuable stores of cinnamon and pepper, all these had been burnt or destroyed. Little remained to pay the cost of the expedition and nothing for the upkeep of the garrison of three thousand men left behind under D. Pedro de Meneses.

Most of the trade which had flowed through the town while it was in Arab hands dried up. It was channelled into other ports along the north African coast. Individual members of the garrison might enrich themselves by plundering farms in the surrounding countryside or by successful piracy in the Straits, a gentlemanly occupation with its own rules. A few merchants might make profitable investments in the trans-Saharan trade. But the King gained no financial advantages from his victory: indeed, far from adding to his revenues, the maintenance of the garrison placed an additional strain on his resources.

Yet his triumph added greatly to his prestige. It certainly surprised his contemporaries and in the long run may not unreasonably be regarded as a turning-point in history. It was nearly eight hundred years since the standards of Islam had erupted from the deserts of Arabia to overrun the decadent empires of Persia and Byzantium. Behind the armies, Arab merchants had moved in to gather into their hands the strands of commerce over a vast area: the caravan routes to China and India, the ports of North Africa, the oases of the Sahara, the shipping of the Indian Ocean and the Persian Gulf, all were under their control.

The forces of the Crusades had been contemptuously repelled.

Although the Ottoman Turks would bite yet deeper into eastern Europe and the fall of Constantinople in 1453 would bring about the final collapse of the Byzantine Empire, by the capture of Ceuta Christianity had launched its first successful counter-attack against Islam. It had been mounted, not by one of the important nations whose kings had led and whose knights had sustained the burden of the Crusades, but by a small, unrecognized and inconsiderable country on the western extremities of the continent. Yet it was, as it turned out, a curtain-raiser to the domination of Europe over Africa and Asia which was to last for more than four hundred years.

3

The Background to the Discoveries

In 1419 or 1420, less than five years after the fall of Ceuta, a Portuguese expedition set sail from the port of Lagos, bound for the unknown south. It was the first halting step in the long series of adventures which was to lead, nearly eighty years later, to the discovery of a sea-way to India by Vasco da Gama.

The traditional explanation for these events was that the trade routes to the Far East had been cut by the Muslims, that the Portuguese decided to outflank Islam and reach the Indies by sailing round southern Africa and that it was Henry the Navigator who was responsible for setting this plan in motion and, during his lifetime, for carrying it out. At most, all three of these notions are only half-truths.

Although history has given most of the credit for begetting the voyages of discovery to D. Henrique, there seems no doubt that his two elder brothers also played their part and that the contribution of D. Pedro especially has been underestimated. But by the time the story of the early voyages came to be written, both D. Duarte and D. Pedro were dead and disgraced: D. Duarte was held responsible for the calamity at Tangier which clouded his short and unsuccessful reign, and D. Pedro for the civil wars during the minority of Afonso V. D. Henrique, on the other hand, was still alive and had a devoted admirer in his protégé, Gomes Eanes de Azurara, on whose writings most subsequent accounts were largely based.

There is no evidence to show that at first the Portuguese planned to reach the Indies: indeed Azurara, concerned though he was to praise the wisdom and foresight of his master, attributes to him, as will be seen, much more modest aims. But in order to decide what the motives and intentions of the Portuguese actually were, it is important to examine not only what conditions prevailed at the time, but also how they themselves interpreted them.

There had always been three main trade routes from the East to the Mediterranean basin: the first, the long overland journey across the steppes of central Asia from China to the Black Sea; the second, by sea from India to the head of the Persian Gulf and then by way of the Tigris or Euphrates valley to Damascus or Baghdad, to the ports of Asia Minor or the Holy Land; the third, through the Red Sea to Egypt and the cities of Cairo and Alexandria. It is true that 'the Golden Journey to Samarkand' was often interrupted, for it lay through the homelands of the Mongol hordes of Genghis Khan and Timurlane. But in the mid-thirteenth century, the era of the *pax mongolica*, visitors from Europe were often able to cross central Asia in safety, and Marco Polo was only one of a number of merchants, explorers and missionaries to do so. Under such Caliphs as Haroun-el-Rashid, Baghdad was a fabulous market for commerce from all parts of the world, and it was only when the Arab dynasty of the Abbasids was over-thrown by the fanatical Seljuk Turks that trading became more difficult and dangerous. But throughout these disturbances the southern route remained open, to be finally closed only when the Ottoman Turks invaded Egypt in 1517, twenty years after Vasco da Gama had reached India by sea.

It was not so much the Arabs, enthusiastic traders them-selves, who prevented the merchants of western Europe from sharing in the profits of the trade with the Far East, but the city-states of northern Italy and especially Venice and Genoa. Sometimes with the dispensation of the Pope for trading with the infidel, and sometimes without, the citizens of these two great republics carried their wares on their own ships from their bases and settlements in the Black Sea and the eastern Mediterranean and distributed them throughout Europe.

It was clearly neither possible nor desirable to try to break the monopoly of the Venetians and Genoese by direct action, but it may well be, in discussions of which there is no record, D. Henrique and his brothers considered whether the sources of their prosperity might not be reached by some other route. For the list of merchandise which trickled into Europe from the East at the beginning of the fifteenth century makes stupendous reading: gold and silver; diamonds and pearls; sapphires, rubies and topaz; carpets and horses; iron, lead and saltpetre; ivory, amber, jade and porcelain; silks and cottons; incense, myrrh and musk; ebony, sandalwood, lacquers and dyes; pepper, ginger, cinnamon, cloves and nutmeg.

But the princes would have found that information about the coveted regions of the East was hard to come by and that what was known about southern 'Ethiopia' was even more fragmentary and inconclusive. It was by no means certain that the Indies could be reached by sea. Those, like the Venetians and the Genoese, who profited from the tales which travellers such as Marco Polo brought back, did their best to keep their knowledge to themselves, as the Portuguese were to do in the years to come. The most fruitful sources of information were private libraries, especially those in the possession of wealthy Arab merchants: they set great store by their collections of manuscripts which included not only the works of their own famous geographers, mathematicians, pharmacists and astrologers, but also translations from the Greek of books which might otherwise have been altogether lost.

Fortunately, there were important libraries close at hand, for since the fall of the Abbasids, the focus of Arab wealth and culture had shifted westwards from Baghdad, and the Moorish cities of Spain, such as Córdoba, Granada and Seville, were at this time among the most civilized places on earth[1]. One can imagine the scholarly D. Duarte sending for copies and translations of Greek and Arab writers to add to his own growing collection of books, meticulously combing them for precious scraps of information which would help his brothers' plans and trying to separate the dragons and dog-headed men of fantasy from the silkworms and pearl divers of fact.

D. Duarte may perhaps have had access to the writings of al-Masudi and Idrisi and even to those of Ibn Batuta, the great traveller whose adventures had been recorded seventy years before on the instructions of the King of Fez. All three described the shores of the Indian Ocean in some detail and by the end of the century that part of the world was sufficiently well known for da Gama to be more or less certain where he was going and what sort of people he was likely to meet. But although Arab seamen had sailed their dhows up and down the east coast of Africa since before the time of Christ, they never ventured beyond the limits of the monsoons in the neighbourhood of Madagascar, and none of them had anything to say about the mystery which surrounded southern Africa. A student of this problem would have had to rely on Greek authors who had lived more than a thousand years before.

Herodotus, writing in the fifth century B.C., told how the Pharaoh Necho sent a Phoenician crew southward through the Arabian Sea to the Southern Ocean and how

after three years they returned to Egypt by way of the
Pillars of Hercules. 'These men', adds Herodotus, 'made
a statement which I do not myself believe, for they said
that, as they sailed on a westerly course along the southern
coast of Libya [Africa], they had the sun on their right,
that is, to the north of them[2].' Four centuries later, Strabo,
whose *Geography* has survived almost in its entirety,
recorded the story of how Eudoxus claimed to have found
on the east coast of Africa the figurehead of a wrecked
galley from Cadiz[3]. In the *Periplus of the Erythrean Sea*, a
guide for sailors written in the first century A.D., the
author states that 'beyond the town of Rhapta the unex-
plored coast curves away to the west and mingles with the
Western Ocean'[4].

By the middle of the fourteenth century many cartographers, including the Majorcan school to whom the
Kings of Aragon gave their patronage, had accepted the
view that there was indeed a sea-way to India round
southern Africa. In the Catalan Atlas of 1375, prepared for
Charles the Wise of France by the Majorcan Jew, Abraham
Cresques, Africa begins for the first time to bear some
resemblance to its true shape. But with the persecution of
the Jews in Aragon and its dependencies this flicker of
modernity was soon put out. It was as yet too soon to
question openly the traditional concept of geography which
had long been sacrosanct in medieval Europe. The official
doctrine of the Church was based on the *mappa-mundi*, the
'wheel map', which placed Jerusalem in the centre of the
inhabited world with the continents disposed symetrically
round it. The discovery of Ptolemy's *Geography*, recently
translated into Latin from a Greek text preserved by the
Arabs, seemed to support the opinions of the traditionalists.
It certainly refuted the ideas of the Majorcan school. For
Ptolemy thought that Africa and southern Asia were joined

by a barrier of land which made of the Indian Ocean a land-locked sea.

Even if this information had all been readily available, it would have been difficult to draw any very definite conclusions from it. There seems, therefore, no reason to doubt the evidence of Azurara and the other chroniclers, who do not mention the Indies, but clearly state that the objective of the early voyages was Guinea.

Azurara lists six reasons which led D. Henrique to seek to reach Guinea by sea: he wished to know with certainty what lay beyond Cape Bojador; he hoped to profit by trade with lands yet to be discovered; to find out the power of the Moors for the greater security of Portugal; to seek a Christian king to help him in his struggle against Islam; to convert unbelievers to Christianity, and lastly, to fulfil his horoscope which foretold that he would be engaged in important and propitious conquests in lands which were hidden from other men[5].

At Ceuta the three young princes had taken part in a feat of arms which had resounded over Europe, but it soon became apparent that they had done no great harm to the empire of the Moors and had gained no substantial commercial advantages. Yet it was surely God's will that they should continue to give battle to the enemies of Christendom and to embarrass and destroy them by any means in their power; for His honour and glory, they must seek to save poor souls from purgatory or worse and bring them the comfort of the Holy Faith; moreover, it was past enduring that the ungodly should so flourish and deny to poor Christian merchants a share in the profits they so shamelessly enjoyed.

It seems likely, in the light of future events, that at first

D. Henrique may have favoured attacks on other Moorish strongholds in North Africa such as Tangier and Arzila. But his brothers would have pointed out that by now the enemy would be on their guard and that a frontal attack would now be most unlikely to succeed, even if the King could be persuaded to agree to such an expensive undertaking. To challenge the Moors indirectly would be much more satisfactory.

D. Henrique had been appointed Governor of Ceuta by his father, with responsibility for the maintenance of the fortress and its garrison. This enabled him to visit the city from time to time and cross-question its inhabitants. From them he would have learnt of their special interest in the Saharan trade; how for centuries past caravans of camels had crossed the desert by well-marked routes from oasis to oasis until they reached the river Niger which lay beyond; how they carried textiles and beads, but mostly they loaded their camels with salt from Taghaza in the northern Sahara, and how they brought back ivory, negro slaves and gold from the markets of Timbuktu and other cities in the Niger kingdom of Mali.

All this agreed with what could be learnt from other sources. In 1324, Mansa Musa, King of Mali, had gone on a pilgrimage to Mecca. He took with him a hundred camels laden with gold to give to the poor: in attendance on him were five hundred slaves, each of whom carried a staff of gold four pounds in weight. The fame of his wealth and generosity dazzled even the sophisticated citizens of Cairo and spread throughout the Mediterranean world. Ibn Batuta visited Mali and the city of Timbuktu and describes them in his book. In the Catalan Atlas, a negro monarch sits on his throne beside the Niger with the inscription, 'This negro lord is called Mussa Melly, king of the negroes of Ginyia. He is the richest and most noble lord because of the abundance of gold which is found in his country.'

The gold of Guinea was the prize which glittered before the eyes of the Portuguese. But since the powerful kingdom of Fez still lay between them and the caravan routes which led across the Sahara, they could only hope to reach it by sea. But even this was an enterprise so hazardous that it had scarcely ever been attempted before.

The coast of Africa was only clearly known as far as Cape Não, so called, men said, because those who ventured beyond it would not return. Between Cape Não and Cape Bojador, the hot, barren coast, beset with shoals, was vaguely charted. The Canaries, off the coast between the two capes, had been known since classical times when they were called the 'Fortunate Isles'. During the fourteenth century they had been frequently visited by Genoese and Catalan sailors and it is possible that as early as 1291 the Vivaldi brothers from Genoa called there before they sailed away southwards into the Atlantic, never to be seen again. At the turn of the century Jean de Bétancourt took possession of the islands in the name of the King of Castile and established colonies on two of them. Beyond the Canaries lay the 'lost' islands of the west, lost in the sense that those who came upon them by chance could not expect to find them again with the aids to navigation then at their disposal. But few captains would willingly endanger their ships in the *Mar Tenebroso*, nor face its fierce storms and mountainous seas. It was widely believed that beyond Cape Bojador the sea boiled and there were whirlpools to entrap and swallow the unwary sailor.

Yet, if the Greeks were to be believed, a voyage to Guinea, though difficult, was not impossible. There were several references in classical authors to such journeys: none of them mentioned torrid heat or whirlpools. In addition to the expedition of Pharaoh Necho's Phoenician captain, which has already been mentioned, Herodotus tells of an attempt by a certain Sataspes to sail round Africa[6]. He followed the coast southwards for many months and reported that at the most southerly point he reached the inhabitants were pygmies, wearing clothes of palm leaves, who fled into the hills at their approach. But Sataspes and his men seized some of their cattle for food. Herodotus also mentions the curious custom of the 'silent trade', which the Portuguese were to hear over and over again in various forms. 'The Carthaginians', he says, 'also tell us that they trade with a race of men who live in a part of Libya beyond the Pillars of Hercules. On reaching that country, they unload their goods, arrange them tidily along the beach and return to their boats and light a fire. Seeing the smoke, the natives come down to the shore, place on the ground a certain quantity of gold in exchange for the goods and retire to a distance. The Carthaginians then come ashore and look at the gold, and, if they think it represents a fair price for their wares, they take it and go away. If, on the other hand, it seems too little, they go back on board and wait and the natives come and add to the gold until the Carthaginians are satisfied. There is perfect honesty on both sides: the Carthaginians never touch the gold until it equals in value what they have offered for sale: the natives never touch the goods until the gold has been taken away[7].'

In his *Natural History*, Pliny included the story of Hanno, whose exploits were recorded on a monument at Carthage until the Romans destroyed the city in 146 B.C. Hanno was sent with a fleet of galleys to found colonies beyond the Pillars of Hercules. His task completed, he continued on his way southwards until he reached a river full of hippopotamus and crocodile where the people spoke a language which his interpreters could not understand. Far beyond this they found a fiery mountain, which they called the Chariot of the Gods, and a land where the men and women were covered with hair[8].

So what little was known of the land of Guinea rested on the testimony of men long since dead.

D. Henrique hoped to convert unbelievers to Christianity, but it is not at all clear what kind of men he expected his captains to find when the coasts of Guinea had been reached. He knew that the rulers of Mali were, or had been, Muslims, for Mansa Musa had gone on the pilgrimage to Mecca. He also knew, presumably, that some eighty years before Mali had begun to lose its supremacy to the Songhor dynasty founded by Sonni Ali. But he must have seen that the negro slaves, brought across the Sahara with the camel caravans, were very different folk from the Moors of North Africa; he would have realized also that they were pagans and supposed that in the outlying districts of the Songhor empire, among her neighbours, he would find virgin soil for his missionary work. But it is very doubtful whether he could have foreseen the wide diversity of cultures, languages and customs which his sailors would encounter.

He hoped also, according to Azurara, to find a Christian king to help him in his struggle against Islam. There had long been talk of a powerful Christian ruler whose realm lay somewhere in Asia or Africa beyond the frontiers of Islam. Later in the century, this ruler, Prester John of the Indies, came to be identified with the Emperor of Ethiopia, but at this time no one knew for certain where his kingdom lay and Ethiopia was an inexact term applied to the whole of Africa south of the Sahara.

One more geographical misconception was to plague the Portuguese. The Niger, the great river which lay to the south of the desert, was supposed to be a branch of the Nile and to flow from east to west. The mystery of the Niger was not finally cleared up until the beginning of the nineteenth century and it was assumed that, if it did indeed flow from east to west, it must emerge somewhere in the Atlantic. If this was so, it could be used to reach the kingdom of Songhor and the golden market of Tungubutu (Timbuktu) from the sea and to outflank the Arab trade-routes across the desert. It might even be possible to follow this highway across the breadth of Africa to the neighbourhood of the Arabian Sea.

Down the Atlantic coast of North Africa the prevailing winds were the north-east trades and the current set steadily in the same direction. Beyond Cape Não the land was inhospitable, a hot, sandy waste, bare of vegetation, which shimmered in the heat and stretched inland, flat and uncompromising, far beyond the limits of human sight. There were few good anchorages and dangerous shoals ran out into the ocean from bleak capes: apart from a few nomads, the region was uninhabited; there was no food and no fresh water was to be had. A ship which was large enough to carry its own provisions for several weeks would, in good weather, meet no great difficulties on its outward voyage, but, until the Portuguese learnt the secret of the wide detour into mid-ocean to pick up the westerlies, the return journey, against wind and current, was always difficult and chancy.

Before the development of the caravel, the tools at D. Henrique's disposal were inadequate for the task he had set himself. There were, of course, many ocean-going ships in Portugal, not only the merchantmen which visited Flanders and England, but the fishing boats which had for centuries past sailed in and out of the west coast ports. These *barchas* were single-masted square-rigged cogs, sturdy enough to ride out rough weather, but unhandy except in a following wind and ill-equipped to beat off a lee shore. They seldom ventured far out of sight of land, ran for shelter in a storm or a contrary wind and in poor visibility felt their way into the ports and estuaries of northern Europe with lead and line.

On the other hand, ship owners in the Mediterranean relied on galleys or feluccas. Though more at home in sheltered waters, galleys had frequently appeared in the Atlantic since the time of the Norsemen. In addition to the war galleys of Castile which had descended on the towns of southern England in the thirteen-seventies, every year the 'great galleys' of Venice, three-masted merchantmen with oars, carried cargoes of spices and other goods to the northern markets. The Genoese and Catalans had used galleys for their early expeditions to the Canaries, but they were really far too light and frail for prolonged ocean voyages and they were so heavily manned for their size that they could not carry provisions for any length of time.

Arab feluccas, with the triangular sails and raked masts which they had borrowed from the dhows of the Indian Ocean, were also a familiar sight in the southern ports of Spain and Portugal. Though small and lightly built, they could, with their lateen rig, sail much closer to the wind than any square-rigged ship and this was an advantage which the Portuguese were later to put to good use.

The mariner's compass, which the Arabs had borrowed from the Chinese, was already in general use in Europe by the beginning of the fifteenth century. Pilots throughout the Mediterranean area were provided with *portulana*, charts criss-crossed with lines which represented compass-bearings between prominent landmarks. Valuable as these *portulana* were for coastal navigation or for enclosed waters, they had only limited use on the high seas where pilots had to rely on dead reckoning. The invention of the astrolabe made it possible to calculate latitude from the height above the horizon of the Pole Star, but such calculations were inaccurate, as the length of a degree was not precisely known. Navigators had still to appreciate and allow for magnetic variation and, since there was no known way of determining longitude, an ocean pilot could only be certain of reaching his destination by first sailing into the correct latitude and then turning either due east or due west.

Under the circumstances it will be seen that, even if their superstitious fears could be allayed, there was still much to be done before D. Henrique could reasonably ask his captains to embark on voyages of discovery into the wastes of the Atlantic.

4

The Noble Generation

In the early fifteenth century many young men of noble birth were still content to sell their services to the highest bidder and range over Europe on warlike expeditions in search of 'honour' and plunder. But the talented young princes of Portugal, educated under the keen eye of their mother, were capable of digesting more solid fare. Their father was concerned to see that his three elder sons at any rate were suitably employed. In addition to the appointment of D. Henrique as Governor of Ceuta, he gave D. Duarte charge of the internal affairs of his kingdom and employed D. Pedro as his ambassador-extraordinary, sending him on a tour of the capitals of Europe.

It may have been his mandate in Ceuta and his need for a convenient base from which he could discharge those responsibilities which first stirred D. Henrique's interest in the Algarve, the most southerly province of Portugal. It was a remote and neglected region, so steeped in Arabic tradition that the courtyards and chimney stacks, underground cisterns and irrigation works, which the Arabs first introduced, still survive even to this day. Yet its climate was amiable and its orchards flourishing. In the gaps in its sandstone cliffs, its little harbours, Lagos, Faro and the rest, bred a race of hardy fishermen and kept in touch with the outside world by providing a refuge in bad weather for ships from the Mediterranean heading for northern Europe. West of Lagos, the sheltered valleys give way to wind-swept open downland, until, in the extreme south-west corner of Europe, Cape St. Vincent thrusts its head into the Atlantic. It is so called because the guardians of the saint's relics, in flight from the Moors in Spain, were said to have been shipwrecked nearby and to have struggled ashore to bury their precious burden on the rocky cape. Here the long Atlantic rollers beat ceaselessly on the cliffs and there is nothing beyond but the open sea. The Romans called the Cape '*Sacro Promontorio*', from which the village of Sagres, a few miles to the east, is generally thought to have taken its name.

It is part of the legend of Henry the Navigator that he came to Sagres soon after the fall of Ceuta and spent there most of the rest of his life, only breaking his seclusion when urgent affairs of state called him away; that from Sagres he organized the voyages of discovery and dispatched his captains in ships built in his own yards, and that he founded there a School of Navigation at which he gathered around him cartographers, astronomers, mathematicians, ship-wrights and pilots from all over Europe. In fact he did not begin to build his *Vila* at Sagres for more than twenty years after he first came to the Algarve. In the meanwhile he seems to have divided his time between a farm he owned at Raposeira, some miles away inland, the nearby hermitage of Nossa Senhora de Guadelupe and a house in Lagos, the port from which many of the expeditions sailed. Nor did he spend by any means all of his time in the south, for he had many preoccupations which required his presence elsewhere. Both the garrison at Ceuta and voyages of discovery needed money and, since they were not at first an attractive investment, the only source of money was the King and the gifts of land and offices which he could bestow. Among other things, D. Henrique had been created Duke of Viseu and Administrator of the Order of

Christ and since these appointments yielded his only regular source of income, the financial affairs of the Order and of his own estates needed constant and careful attention.

It is true that as soon as he had something to show for his efforts he did attract foreigners to his service. An early recruit was the distinguished geographer, Jaime Cresques, whose father had produced the Catalan Atlas. Later on the Prince was joined by foreign knights in search of adventure, such as the Dane, Abelhart, and merchants in search of profit, such as the Genoese, Cadamosto. But the idea of a sort of nautical laboratory, where the voyages could be scientifically planned and their results studied, is certainly exaggerated. It is possible that the first experimental caravels were built in the little bay at Sagres so that the secrets of their construction could be preserved, but the first captains were young men of his own household, adventurous but untrained. They sailed from Lagos in traditional *barchas*, manned and equipped from his own revenues and from those of the Order of Christ.

If D. Henrique had expected quick results from his quest for a sea route to Guinea, his patience must have been sadly tried. It was fourteen years before any appreciable progress was made and meanwhile his young commanders seemed more concerned with enriching themselves at the expense of Arab merchantmen in known waters than with risking their lives in the 'Green Sea of Shades' beyond Cape Bojador.

But it is more likely his captains did exactly what was expected of them and that D. Henrique hoped to use the profits of these corsairs to pay for a thorough exploration of the western isles. Later on, Madeira and the Açores were to prove invaluable as ports of call, especially for crews returning from Guinea and beyond by the Atlantic circuit; it is to be presumed that this is what D. Henrique had in mind from the start. If this is so, the years from 1420 to 1434 were by no means wasted.

It had long been known that the mythology of Atlantis, Antilia, the Isle of the Seven Cities and so on, had some foundation in fact. Besides the Canaries, several genuine islands had been visited by sailors driven off their course in storms. But it was through D. Henrique that the positions of these islands were for the first time accurately fixed or as accurately as the instruments of the period would allow so that in future they could easily be located and used as ports of call.

D. Henrique would have liked to have taken possession of one of the Canaries, but his father would not allow him to do so for fear of offending Castile. The islands were, in any case, inhabited by a fierce, indigenous race who greeted strangers by hurling rocks at them, 'for', says Azurara, 'stones are exceedingly plentiful on the islands and the people make good use of them'. So the first success, in 1420 or thereabouts, was the discovery of the small island of Porto Santo. Two of his young men, João Gonçalves Zarco and Tristão Vaz, put into its harbour for shelter. They found it uninhabited and treeless, but apparently fertile. Since they felt that they had been able to calculate its position more or less exactly, they offered to return there with a group of colonists. They were joined in their venture by Bartolemeu Perestrello, into whose family Columbus was afterwards to marry, and set out to pioneer the overseas empire of Portugal. Unfortunately Perestrello had been presented with a doe rabbit which littered on the way out. 'Having built themselves shelters', Azurara records, 'they set the rabbit and her little ones at liberty so that they might breed. And they multiplied so fast that before long they covered the whole island and the men could plant nothing which was not at once eaten or destroyed.'

The three adventurers returned home to tell their troubles to the Prince, but he, by no means despondent, sent them out once more to investigate a mysterious cloud which they reported hanging motionless over the sea to the south of Porto Santo. This cloud, they found, concealed another, larger island, so covered with vegetation that Zarco and his men had to cut their way inland with machetes. Because of the abundance of trees they called their new discovery Madeira. There were no people on it, but according to one member of the party they found there an inscription in Latin, which read, 'Here came the Englishman Machin, borne by a storm, and here lies the woman who came with him'. Robert Machin is said to have fled from England about 1345, with Anne Dorset, to escape from a marriage which her father had arranged for her.

D. Henrique now granted the lordship of Porto Santo and its rabbits to Perestrello and divided the island of Madeira between Zarco and Tristão Vaz. He gave them cattle, sheep and poultry to take with them and thereafter the island was regularly visited by Portuguese ships in need of repairs or of food and water. When the Genoese merchant Cadamosto called there in 1455 there were already four settlements and eight hundred inhabitants, prosperous farmers who were already growing rich from the profits on their vines and sugar-cane. But even this fertile colony had its early troubles, for Zarco's men found it a gruelling task to clear the land for their plantations. In attempting to burn out an area of bush in the valley of Funchal, they kindled a fire which destroyed nearly all they had so far achieved and which smouldered under the heaps of ashes for seven years. At the height of the fire the colonists had to shelter from the heat up to their necks in the sea. On Porto Santo there was still a multitude of rabbits more than a century later: João de Barros records that in his own time a landing party killed more than three thousand in a single day.

The nine islands of the Açores were accurately charted by Gonçalvo Velho between 1427 and 1432. For the time being D. Henrique did not attempt to colonize them, but contented himself with landing herds of cattle and flocks of sheep. Since there was no wild life except the falcons which gave the islands their name, these animals looked after themselves and provided another useful source of food for passing ships.

Meanwhile D. Pedro had set out on his tour of the capitals of Europe. He seems to have left home in the late summer of 1425 and been away for rather more than three years. The reasons for his journey are not precisely clear. He was a handsome young prince who had taken part in a celebrated military exploit. He was an honoured and popular guest and his hosts hastened to arrange banquets and tournaments for him wherever he went. But it was much more than an exercise in chivalry. His father needed friends and allies and wished to stress that Porgual was not a rebellious province of Castile, but a truly independent kingdom. D. Pedro himself was eager to learn all he could about contemporary Europe, especially its pattern of commerce and its relations with the Muslim world. He hoped in this way to forward the plans which he and his brothers had in mind. He was also under an obligation to Sigismund, King of Hungary and future Holy Roman Emperor who, in 1418, had appointed him Marquis of Treviso, a small territory to the north of the Adriatic which was in dispute between himself and the Venetian Republic.

Early in the sixteenth century a romantic narrative was woven round the travels of D. Pedro by the Spanish writer Gomez de Santisteban. In the tradition of Sir John Mandeville, the Knights of the Round Table and El Cid, the story is embroidered with heroic episodes and geographical fantasies to the taste of the period. It takes the Prince to Troy and Babylon (Baghdad), Jerusalem and southern India: it introduces him to the Ottoman Sultan, to Prester John and to the Nestorian Christians whose ancestors were said to have been converted to Christianity by St. Thomas. But Santisteban's tale was fiction, not fact, and the realities of D. Pedro's travels were very different.

He sailed first to England to see his Lancastrian kinsmen. The records show that in October 1425 he was able to assist in resolving a dispute, the first of many, between his step-uncle Henry Beaufort, Bishop of Winchester, and Humphrey, Duke of Gloucester, over the custody of the child-king Henry VI. He would have felt himself very much at home in England: tall and broad-shouldered, his hair and beard tinged with red, he took after his mother's family and might well have been mistaken for an Englishman. His companion and great friend, D. Álvaro Vaz de Almeda, had fought at Agincourt and had been made Count of Avranches after the battle. Both he and the Prince were afterwards to be appointed Knights of the Garter.

In December 1425 D. Pedro moved on to Bruges. In this great commercial city, where the Portuguese had a long-established 'Factory', he could have examined the network of trade which radiated from it all over northern Europe. He would certainly have visited the city's famous library. He may well have opened the negotiations which were to lead, four years later, to the marriage of his sister Isabel to the ruler of Bruges, Philip the Good, Duke of Burgundy, who had recently lost his second wife.

From Bruges, D. Pedro journeyed across central Europe to Hungary. He spent two years at the court of Sigismund and in 1427 took part in the future Emperor's campaign against the Ottoman Turks. He was thus able to judge for himself how serious was the threat to Christendom in south-east Europe, how little interest and assistance Sigismund was receiving from his Christian colleagues and how great was the need for unity in the face of the common enemy. D. Pedro does not seem to have fought against the heretical Hussites in Bohemia as tradition suggests. Nor, apparently, did he visit the Marquisate which Sigismund had bestowed on him until he passed through Treviso on his way to Venice and what was to prove the most important part of his journey.

Venice in 1428 was at the height of her wealth and power: the palaces of her rich merchant-bankers lined the canals and lagoons; her ships traversed the Mediterranean from Smyrna and Alexandria to the Straits of Gibraltar; her 'great galleys' carried her trade to the ports of England and Flanders; her agents were to be found in all the commercial cities of Europe and the Near East; her markets overflowed with exotic luxuries. Though from time to time the Pope might threaten her merchants with excommunication for trafficking with the infidel, they seldom took account of it. There was no place on earth where more could be learnt about trade and the Muslim world and no place where such a feat as the capture of Ceuta would be better appreciated. D. Pedro was given a civic welcome and provided with guides to show him the wonders of the city.

His visit was recorded by Antonio Morosini. After describing the celebrations held in D. Pedro's honour, he tells us how the young Prince 'went to all parts of the Arsenal and every corner of the shipyards. There he saw more than sixty galleys on the stocks; he assisted in their

construction and went on board several which were already
launched. He took note of the arrangement of their masts,
their rigging and their sails. He took part in setting masts
in every section of the naval yards and afterwards walked
through the docks, by a route a long way from the Citadel,
to see the ships anchored in the port. . . . On the next day,
accompanied by the Doge himself, he visited the market,
observing the shops of all kinds, full of spices, sugar,
velvets, cloth of gold, silk and other materials. He passed
through the street of the goldsmiths, admiring all the
jewellery and precious stones, pearls, necklaces, rings, dishes
and garments of all colours for men and women[1].'

D. Pedro left Venice with a copy of the travels of Marco
Polo in his luggage and with an up-to-date map of the
world which the Doge had given him. But even now he was
not ready to go home. He went by way of Padua to
Florence. In both these cities the universities were flourishing and in Florence, under the patronage of the Medicis,
scholars such as Toscanelli were already engaged on the
studies which were to free geography from the shackles of
classical and ecclesiastical tradition. Their theories were not
to become widely known for another ten years or more,
until after the Council of Florence. But an intelligent and
enquiring visitor might have learnt that they now believed
that the world was round and that they could even calculate
its approximate dimensions: that the lands of Cathay and
Cipangu could, therefore, in theory be reached by sailing
west across the Atlantic, but the distance was so great that
the venture might, in practice, prove to be impossible.
D. Pedro would have been disappointed to learn that they
had nothing new to tell him about the southward extent of
the African continent.

Pope Martin was a protégé of Sigismund. No doubt on
that account D. Pedro was sympathetically received in

King João I entertaining John of Gaunt, probably at Oporto, 1386

Marriage of Philippa of Lancaster, daughter of John of Gaunt

Rome. The immediate result of his visit was a Papal Bull which granted to the princes of Portugal the privilege of 'Annointment' and so recognized the independent status of the royal house. His relations with Rome remained good to the end of his life. Both Martin and his successors supported the Portuguese claim to monopoly in African exploration and on several occasions granted the proceeds of taxes on church property to help defray the cost of their expeditions.

It may well be that D. Pedro had originally intended to visit the Holy Land, as his half-brother, the Count of Barcelos, had done twenty years before. But it is quite certain that he never did so. Somewhere on his travels he would have heard that D. Duarte intended to get married and it was perhaps this news which made him change his mind and decide to go home. His brother's wedding, of course, would make a great difference to his own prospects, for his father was old and D. Duarte himself physically not very robust. Whatever his reasons, D. Pedro arrived in Barcelona early in July. But even now he did not hurry himself, for he found plenty to interest him in Aragon. The Kingdom had been a power in the Mediterranean for many years; it had been the home of an important school of geography since the middle of the previous century; its sailors had visited the Canaries and perhaps also the unknown coast of West Africa before the idea had even occurred to the Portuguese; only the year before an embassy from the mysterious land of Ethiopia had visited King Afonso. D. Pedro would have wished to hear as much as he could about all these things, with the result that he hardly left himself time to travel across Castile and pay his respects to King Juan II. On 22nd September 1428 D. Duarte was married at Coimbra to D. Leonor of Aragon. His brother had arrived in the city only the day before.

The chroniclers do not tell us what use D. Pedro made of the ideas and information he had gathered on his travels and we can only guess what effect they may have had on his future actions and opinions. It can safely be assumed that he was deeply impressed with the strength and virility of the Islamic kingdoms and realized how unprofitable it would be to deliver a frontal attack at any points on the shores of the Mediterranean. For the rest of his life he was to oppose all schemes for military adventures in North Africa and to encourage his brother to concentrate on trade and exploration. He was convinced that the Muslim world must be outflanked and alliances sought with Christian kings and peoples who lived beyond it to the south and east. But for such a policy to succeed, a way must be found to reach these distant lands by sea and the first step was to overcome the obstacle of Cape Bojador.

D. Henrique's solution to this problem was to risk the displeasure of the King of Castile and to establish an advanced base in the Canaries. In spite of his father's misgivings, in 1424 Fernão de Castro had attempted to seize Grand Canary on his behalf. He argued that the Castilians had only established a valid claim by occupation to the two islands of Lançarote and Forteventura. But the Castilians, who themselves laid claim to the whole group, reacted strongly to the activities of the Portuguese: they eventually persuaded the Pope to support them and in 1436 Eugene IV issued a Bull in which he warned the King of Portugal not to risk war with his neighbour by any further interference in the islands[2].

D. Pedro agreed with the Pope. War with Christian Castile was a waste of scarce resources which had much better be deployed against the Moors. He advocated the provision of better ships and equipment so that the physical difficulties of long sea voyages could more easily to overcome. Though we cannot be certain, there seems little doubt that the design of the caravels was inspired by his visit to the shipyards of Venice.

Although the search for the lost Atlantic islands had been successful, D. Henrique had still made no progress along the coast of Africa. The fear of the unknown, exaggerated by sailors' talk in the taverns of Portuguese ports, still gripped his men and Cape Bojador was a hazard which no one yet had the courage to face. In 1433 the Prince fitted out another ship and gave command of it to Gil Eanes, a young squire of his household. But he also lost his nerve off the fateful Cape and, instead of doing what his master had instructed him, turned aside to raid the Canaries and bring some of the islanders home as prisoners. D. Henrique began to lose patience: he fitted out the same ship once more and spoke very seriously to Gil Eanes. 'My son,' he said, 'you know that I have brought you up since you were a small boy and that I am confident that you will serve me well. For this reason I have chosen you to be captain of this ship to go to Cape Bojador and discover what lies beyond. You cannot there meet any dangers so great that the hope of reward may not yet be greater. In truth I marvel at the fears which have taken hold of you and all the others of my servants. If these tales which are spread around had even the smallest authority, I would not blame you. But you have listened to the gossip of sailors who know only the ports of Flanders and other countries where traders have always gone: they cannot use a compass and they know nothing of charts. You go your way and forget what they have said. By the grace of God you will return from your voyage laden with honours and profit.'

From this voyage of 1434 Gil Eanes brought back only

a handful of dry leaves and news of a barren coast without trace of man or beast. But in sailing past Cape Bojador through calm waters, the young captain had laid a bogey. The worthless plants, the 'Roses of St. Mary', as he called them, were a most welcome gift to bring home to his master.

Though they were still cautious, D. Henrique's crews now brought home some new intelligence from every voyage. In 1435 Gil Eanes and Afonso Gonçalves took their ships fifty leagues beyond the Cape and found the footprints of men and camels in the sand. By 1436, the Prince was already deep in preparations for a new descent on North Africa, with Tangier as its chosen target: he yet had time to fit out another ship for a voyage towards the south. Seventy leagues beyond the furthest point he had reached in the previous year, Gonçalves came to the mouth of a wide river. He called it Rio de Ouro, for this surely was the river, which, according to the tales of Moorish travellers, lay close to the source of the gold of Guinea. Here the captain disembarked and sent two young men on horseback to explore. They followed the river for several miles, until suddenly they came on a party of nineteen natives; the two horsemen charged them, but they, terrified by this apparition of strange animals and stranger men with white faces wearing extraordinary clothes, incontinently fled into the bush. Neither then nor next morning could they be found again and Gonçalves had to be content with collecting what belongings they had left behind, with their fishing nets spread out to dry on the shore and with the skins of some of the numerous seals which lay basking on the sand-bars at the mouth of the river. So to these two young Portuguese, Heitor Homen and Diogo Lopes, fell the distinction of meeting the first human beings to be seen on the newly-discovered coast of West Africa.

During the last years of his father's long reign, D. Duarte prepared himself after his own fashion for the tasks which lay ahead. From the literature of his own country, from the lives and epistles of the saints, from such of the writings of ancient Greece and Rome as were within his reach, he distilled his own political philosophy, explaining in his book, *Leal Conselhero*, how nobles and clergy, merchants and labourers each had their part to play in society under the King. So that when, on 14th August 1433, the anniversary of his birth and of the battle of Aljubarrota, D. João died at the age of seventy-seven, his son was ready to set to work on the new body of law which would transform Portugal into his ideal state.

D. Duarte was a scholar and philosopher. He was also a man of great integrity, pious and conscientious, with a profound regard for justice and a deep sense of his obligations towards his subjects. But he was also irresolute and unpractical, utterly unsuited to rule over a turbulent medieval kingdom. His natural environment was his library, where, pen in hand, he would try to write himself out of his problems. Peter Quennell has said of Richard II of England that 'he was a master of words who found in the beauty of words an exquisite substitute for thought and action'[3]. D. Duarte was very like his kinsman.

At the time of the Enterprise of Ceuta, D. João had put him in charge of his secretariat, a task for which he was well-suited. At his accession, his brother Pedro, well knowing his limitations, addressed him a letter from Leiria, counselling him to write no more but to follow the policies and precepts of his father.

From the beginning the omens were, quite literally, unfavourable for the new King. Rui de Pina tells us how, on the morning after D. João's death, while he was preparing for the ceremony at which he was to be proclaimed

King, there came to him Master Guedelha, a Jew, his doctor and a learned astrologer, who said, 'I believe, Senhor, that you intend to enter immediately into the royal succession which belongs to you by right. I pray you delay until midday has passed and by so doing, thanks to God, you will do yourself profit. For now the stars are inauspicious: Jupiter is in decline and the positions of the sun and other heavenly bodies are equally infelicitous.'

The Prince replied, 'I well know, Master Guedelha, that of the great love you bear me is born this care for my honour and service: nor do I doubt that astrology is deserving of belief and is one of those sciences which should be permitted and approved. However, what I principally believe is that God is above all things and that all is in His hands and subject to His commands. To Him only therefore do I commend myself and to the well-loved Virgin Mary, His Mother, whose day we celebrate today. With great devotion and due humility, I pray to God that he teaches me, favours me and helps me to govern these His people.'

And Master Guedelha in his turn said, 'Senhor, it surely pleases him that this is so, but if it had not been greatly inconvenient, it would have been better for you to delay.'

And the Prince replied, 'I will not do this, nor ought I to do so, lest it appear that I have no trust in God, nor the faith in Him that I ought to have.'

Then Master Guedelha affirmed that the new King would reign only a few, short years and these would be years of great trouble and distress. And, adds the chronicler, 'they were, as will shortly be told'. In a little more than five years D. Duarte was dead, his high hopes drained away in catastrophe at Tangier.

He gained little credit from the new laws by which he had set such store. The nobility resented the *lei mental*, so called because it was in his father's mind before he died, by which land and titles could only pass through the male line and both must revert to the Crown if there was no son to inherit. By this law he hoped to make good some of the loss to his revenues which D. João's generosity had so seriously diminished. By another he hoped to solve the problem of the Jewish community by offering two-thirds of the family property to any Jew who forsook his own faith for Christianity, but this temptation the Jews ignored.

He could not manage his own relations. His father had unwisely married his two eldest sons into families which were rivals for the throne of Aragon. The Queen, D. Leonor de Aragon, detested D. Isabel de Urgel, D. Pedro's wife, and resented the Prince's influence over her husband. The King's brothers, although they were fond of him and unfailingly loyal, could not feel the deference for him they had felt for their father and did not hesitate to vex him with their problems. D. Fernão, the youngest brother, complained that the revenue from the lands his father had given him was not sufficient to keep up his position and begged permission to seek his fortune abroad. D. Henrique brought forward his long-cherished scheme for a new assault on the Moors in North Africa and suggested that he should take D. Fernão with him.

The King was perplexed: he was reluctant to involve himself in such a chancy affair, nor was he certain that he would gain much from it even if it were successful. He was well aware that the capture of Ceuta had been by no means so profitable to the Crown as had been expected and that the upkeep of the garrison there cost more than he could afford. Yet he could not allow D. Fernão to leave the country for there were many other young *fidalgos* eager to follow his example.

D. Henrique refused to abandon his plans: he persuaded the Pope to issue a Bull of Absolution for those who should die in the forthcoming Crusade[4]. He enlisted the Queen on his side, and she, swayed not so much perhaps by the high-sounding sentiments which D. Henrique expressed as by a desire to cross D. Pedro, made up her devoted husband's mind for him. The new Enterprise would go forward.

The attack on Tangier seemed ill-fated from the start. There was none of the popular enthusiasm which had shown itself before Ceuta. There were few foreign ships to be had because of other wars in northern Europe, so that only six thousand men could be carried over to Africa. The destination of this army was no secret and the Moorish general, Sala-bin-Sala, had plenty of time to make his preparations.

The King grew daily more apprehensive. But D. Henrique was still full of confidence and scarcely listened to the advice which his brother showered on him. 'Make sure', said D. Duarte, 'that when you pitch camp, you extend both flanks to the sea, or, if you do not have enough men to do this, let at least one of the flanks of your army rest on the sea, so that you may be assured of supplies and help and a safe line of retreat if need be.'

On the battlefield D. Henrique showed none of the patience, foresight and commonsense which he was accustomed to devote to his expeditions. Whether because, after his easy success at Ceuta, he despised the Moor as a fighting man; or because he was convinced that believers in the True Faith must of necessity triumph over the infidel; or because, more simply, he lost his head in the heat of battle, he made every possible mistake at Tangier. He moved slowly and ponderously along the coast road from Ceuta; he made three expensive attacks on the walls of the city with inadequate equipment; while he waited for longer ladders and heavier cannon, he wasted more valuable lives on aimless skirmishes; finally, disregarding his orders from the King, he allowed himself to be surrounded by a greatly superior force and cut off from the sea without food or water.

To save the lives of his men, D. Henrique agreed to a truce, Sala-bin-Sala demanded the surrender of Ceuta in return for a safe-conduct, and of D. Fernão who was to be held as a hostage until the cession of the city could be arranged. In deep distress D. Henrique watched his much loved younger brother ride away into captivity. In spite of the truce, he himself and the survivors of his army only reached the safety of the fleet with difficulty, for they were constantly attacked by warrior tribesmen over whom their commander had no control.

D. Fernão never saw Portugal again. He died in prison in Fez in 1443. During the five years of his martyrdom, the negotiations for his release and ransom dragged on. The Portuguese were prepared to make any sacrifice to save his life—except surrender Ceuta.

D. Duarte did not long survive the disaster. He died, some said, of his great sorrow and remorse at the inglorious outcome of the siege. D. Henrique retired to nurse his humiliation at Sagres.

5

The Regency of Dom Pedro

The new King, Afonso V, was only six years old when his father died and trouble at once arose over the Regency. There are many similiarities between the events of Afonso's reign and that of his Lancastrian cousin, Henry VI, who had succeeded to the throne of England in 1422 at an even earlier age. In both kingdoms the Regency was long in dispute; both kings were ineffective and easily dominated; both became involved in unsuccessful and costly foreign wars; in neither case was the struggle for power which boiled around them settled in their lifetime; in England the Wars of the Roses only blew themselves out with the death of Richard III in 1485; in Portugal the threat to the throne was only extinguished with the ruin of the Braganças in 1483-4.

It might have been expected that D. Pedro, the young King's energetic and popular uncle, would have assumed the Regency without question. But after D. Duarte's death, it was found that he had bequeathed both the Regency and the care of his children to his feather-brained Queen, D. Leonor. There were, of course, those who preferred a woman at the head of affairs rather than the strong hand of D. Pedro. Among them was Afonso, Count of Barcelos, the eldest but illegitimate son of João I. At this time the Count was a man of about sixty, a tough medieval baron, with much of his father's shrewdness. But his bastardy had not only excluded him in his youth from the civilizing influences of Queen Philippa's court, but had also debarred him, in his own opinion, from a fair share in the honours which his father had showered on his younger half-brothers after Ceuta. The time had come, he thought, for his position and importance to be properly recognised, and with this in mind he came hurrying south from his estates in Tras-os-Montes to support the widowed Queen and to press for the marriage of his grand-daughter Isabel to the King.

D. Pedro was unwilling to seize power by unconstitutional means, but the citizens of Lisbon supported him to a man. They declared that they would not have a woman for Regent, and a foreigner at that. Nor would the Cortes, who not only offered the Regency to D. Pedro, but maintained that D. Leonor was not even a fit person to look after her own children. After this blow to her hopes, the Queen Mother fled to Castile, where she soon afterwards died. As for the Count of Barcelos, he had already withdrawn to his estates in the north to await a more favourable opportunity. He was not too subdued, however, to beg his 'dearly loved' brother, the Regent, to create him Duke of Bragança. This D. Pedro did with a good grace. But the young King married, not Isabel the grand-daughter of the new Duke, but Isabel, the daughter of the Regent.

D. Henrique had done no more than hover on the outskirts of these disturbances. They had interrupted his work for three years and when they were over he returned thankfully to the Algarve to plan a new series of voyages. He now had, of course, his brother's interest and support and there can be little doubt that the successes of the next few years owned much to the Regent's backing. D. Pedro had already given him permission to colonize the Açores[1] and in a surprisingly short time the colonists of these islands and of Madeira were sending back to Portugal substantial quantities of timber which could be used for ship-building, sugar and wheat, and wine from Malvoisie grapes imported from Cyprus. The Regent now confirmed D. Duarte's grant of the 'royal fifth' from the profits of all voyages and decreed that no expedition could sail beyond Cape Bojador without a licence from the Infante[2]. He also opened negotiations with the Pope which resulted, after his death, in the Bulls of 1450 and 1453, conceding to Afonso V not only all territories already discovered, but all future conquests in the land of Guinea[3].

As yet D. Henrique had little to show for his investments. The proceeds of attacks on Arab merchantmen and the sale of the oil and skins of the seals of the Rio de Ouro by no means covered his expenses. It is true that almost every voyage now added to his knowledge of the geography of the west coast. Year by year he could plot on the charts of the barren coast that stretched so remorselessly southward details of some new bay or headland, some spring or river where fresh water could be obtained, some sheltered anchorage or some shoal or reef which must be avoided. But the cost of his expeditions still had to be largely met from his own pocket or from the revenues of the Order of Christ.

From 1441 onwards, however, he began at last to gain some reward for his perseverance. Where before his captains had seen only footprints in the sand or caught a fleeting glimpse of terrified nomads, they began to find and bring home natives who could be questioned about the people and customs of the lands from which they came and the products and commerce of the interior. His ships, too, would soon put the desert behind them and find themselves in the more fertile and populous regions further south.

Nuno Tristão, who led one of the expeditions of 1441, was entrusted with a vessel of a new design in which he succeeded in reaching Cabo Branco. The chroniclers are silent about the years of experiment which must have gone into the evolution of the caravel. The Portuguese were determined to keep its design a secret for as long as they could, but it is not unreasonable to suppose that work on the prototype was put in hand soon after D. Pedro's return from Venice and that it took twelve years to perfect it. This new kind of ship, which replaced the *barchas* used for the earlier voyages, was soon to become the admiration of all Europe. It was a hybrid. Its hull was modelled on the fishing boats of the western ports, strengthened to withstand the storms of the Atlantic, but its masts, two at first and later three of them, and its lateen rig, were borrowed from the Mediterranean. With its triangular sails, set fore and aft, it could sail close to the wind and so overcome the difficulties of the return voyage from the south. It was fast and handy, well-adapted for nosing in and out of the estuaries and among the shoals of the West African coast. It led the way from the Rio de Ouro to the Great Fish River beyond the Cape of Good Hope. It was only superseded at the end of the century when long ocean passages demanded more space for men and stores and a stronger armament for defence.

Of several contemporary or near contemporary sources which cover this period, Azurara's *Chronicles of Guinea* is the most detailed and in many ways the most valuable. He was a member of D. Henrique's own household; he knew most of those who took part in the adventures he describes; he was often present when they set out on their travels and met them when they returned; he based his narrative on interviews with men who had actually taken part in the voyages, on notes he had made at the time, on the lost *History* of Cerveira and perhaps on an earlier version of his own. Yet in some respects Azurara's book is disappointing. He was especially concerned to sing the praises of his master and the captains of his ships; D. Pedro, who was dead and disgraced by the time he wrote, is only mentioned in passing; his chronology and his geography are often difficult to unravel; he has little to say about the people of Africa and their way of life; far too much of his chronicle is taken up with meticulous and somewhat unappetizing accounts of raids on unsuspecting villages and the capture and murder of defenceless Moors and negroes.

The Venetian, Cadamosto, takes up the story where Azurara leaves off. He sailed on two expeditions under the Portuguese flag and though he is inclined to exaggerate his own part, his *Voyages* are full of interesting details about the people he met, their customs and political organization, their economy and the trade routes of the interior. Another version of the same events was written by Diogo Gomes. He was at one time one of D. Henrique's captains, but he afterwards became Treasurer of the Royal Palace at Sintra. In his old age he related his experiences to the German geographer, Martin Behaim, the maker of the oldest known terrestrial globe. One would say that the old man's memory had failed – he was over eighty – or that Martin Behaim did not report him accurately.

Extra details can be gathered from the *Esmeraldo de Situ Orbis* of Duarte Pacheco, written by command of King Manuel about 1505. This work is not a chronicle, but a guide-book for sailors and traders. Duarte's father had been a close associate of D. Henrique and he himself had served in West Africa as Governor of the fortress of Sao Jorge da Mina and had also spent two years in India. There is additional material in the first book of the *Decadas de Asia,* written by João de Barros in the middle of the next century. But this great prose epic is of more value for the voyages which took place during the later years of Afonso V and the reign of João II, for these are less well-documented.

Although all these writers tell basically the same story, there are many minor discrepancies. From 1441 onwards there were many more expeditions and so more captains and more ships; the sequence of events becomes more difficult to follow. Details assigned to a particular voyage by one author are often placed in a different context or even in a different year by another.

The distinction of bringing home the first captives from beyond Cape Bojador fell to Antão Gonçalves. He had set out to hunt seals. 'Our first task is now completed,' he said when they had loaded their catch, 'but I would like to know if it seems good to you that we should attempt something more to show our loyalty to our master who sent us forth. This night I intend to go on shore with nine chosen men so that we may try to find some of the inhabitants of this land. Since they do not yet know of our arrival here, they should not be gathered together in such strength that we cannot overcome them. And if we could make some of them captive, it would give great satisfaction to our Lord the Infante, for from them he could learn much of the people who live in these parts.'

The little party set out, but though they found traces of men and beasts in the sand, it was not until they were on their way back to their ship after a long and exhausting day in the hot sun that they came on a man, walking naked beside his camel with two spears in his hand. They took him prisoner, together with an old woman whom they surprised on her way to draw water from the river.

It was now clear that on a nearby hill there was an encampment of Moors, too numerous for them to attack. But, as it happened, they were now able to join forces with Nuno Tristão who had arrived at the anchorage in his caravel. D. Henrique had told them to approach in peace whoever they might meet, but with men who fled at the sight of them and who spoke no language they could understand, this was easier said than done. They decided to attack the camp by night: in the skirmish they took ten more prisoners, one of whom, to judge by his dress and demeanour, they supposed to be more important than his fellows.

To D. Henrique this man was indeed a prize. His name was Adahu and he belonged to the Sanhaja Tuareg, whom the Portuguese called Azanegues. He spoke Arabic and had travelled widely over the caravan routes of the Sahara; he had visited the country of the pagan Mandinga, the Kingdom of Mali and the fabulous city of Timbuktu. This city, he explained, lay on the banks of the great river Niger; gold was plentiful there; he had once seen a train of three hundred camels laden with it; but where it came from he did not know for certain; he only knew that it was exchanged for salt by men from the region of Wangara whom the merchants never saw. They left the salt in a customary place and, when they returned some days later, the salt had disappeared and gold had been left in its stead. It was said that the people of Wangara had the heads and tails of dogs. The land of Guinea, of which Wangara was a part, was thickly populated and heavily forested, but of the Empire of Prester John Adahu could tell the Infante nothing, except, perhaps, that it might lie to the south of Egypt.

After some months Adahu began to grow homesick for his own land. He explained to Antão Gonçalves that there were with his tribe many negro slaves and that he would willingly give five or six of them in exchange for his own liberty; and furthermore, there were among his fellow captives, two other young men whose ransom would be worth as much as, or more, than his own. Since by this time D. Henrique had learnt from these Azanegues all that they could usefully tell him, he willingly agreed that Antão Gonçalves should sail again for the Rio de Ouro and take the three captives with him.

According to Azurara, a German knight joined this expedition, the first of many foreigners to serve in a Portuguese ship. If the German was looking for excitement, he was not long in finding it, for the caravel was struck by a storm so violent that the crew gave themselves up for lost. By the grace of God it survived, but it had to return to Portugal to refit.

The second attempt was more successful. Adahu was duly landed and put on parole to go and fetch the slaves for his ransom. But to the great disgust of the Portuguese, he disappeared into the interior and was seen no more. So Gonçalves learnt that the etiquette of chivalry had no meaning among the Azanegues. But he did not go altogether empty away, for he was able to ransom his two other prisoners for ten negroes, a little gold dust, a shield and a great quantity of ostrich eggs, some of which were afterwards served at his master's table.

Some of those who had previously thought that the Infante's projects were a waste of time and money were beginning to change their minds. The first to do so were the citizens of Lagos who were best placed to hear and appraise the latest news. In 1444 they equipped and dispatched the first privately-sponsored expedition, six ships under the command of Lançarote. It sailed, of course, with D. Henrique's permission and blessing.

By this time the Tropic of Cancer and Cabo Branco had been reached and passed; the islands of Arguim and Tider, which lay just north of the twentieth parallel, had been added to the map. Though the mainland was still bare and unpromising there were many more inhabitants among the islands than there had been further north. Most of them were fishermen and their families who lived in clusters of huts near the shore.

Lançarote and his men found the hunting good. They rounded up more than two hundred of these unfortunate folk and shipped them off to Portugal to be sold as slaves. On the day after their arrival at Lagos the first slave market was held in a meadow outside the city. The scene, unfortunately to be repeated in many parts of the world during the next four hundred years, was described in such detail by Azurara that it seems certain that he was there himself.

'Let my tears trouble not my conscience', he wrote, 'for I wept with pity at their sufferings. For what heart, even the hardest, would not be moved by such a gathering. Some bowed their heads, their faces wet with tears; others groaned piteously, lifting their eyes to heaven; others beat their faces with their hands and threw themselves to the ground; yet others wailed in lamentation as is the custom of their country.

'Then, to increase their sufferings the more, there came those who were commanded to divide them and they began to part them one from another in order to put them in groups of equal value. For this, it was necessary to separate children from their parents, women from their husbands and brothers from brothers. No ties of kinship or love could keep them together, each must go where fate drove him. But as soon as they had been led to their appointed place, children who had been snatched from their parents ran quickly back to them and their mothers clasped their offspring in their arms, throwing themselves on the ground and covering them with their bodies, paying no heed to the blows they received.

'And thus, with much difficulty they were at last divided. The field was full of people from the towns, villages and countryside alike who had come for no other purpose than to see this novelty. The Infante was there, on a great horse, riding among his people. He received his share of one fifth like a man who was by no means eager to own great wealth and at once offered it to the Church, for his pleasure was in the thought that these poor souls could be saved from perdition.

'His hopes were not in vain. As soon as these Moors understood our language, they became Christians. And when their masters found they were not hardened in their beliefs like the Moors from North Africa, they treated them as they treated their free servants. Some of the honest widows who bought girl-slaves adopted them as their daughters: others made them heirs to their wealth. I never saw chains on any of these slaves and more than once I have been invited by their owners to witness their baptism or marriage.'

This expedition was hailed as a great success and Lançarote was knighted by D. Henrique at the request of his fellow-captains. It is perhaps worth noting that the steady trickle of Africans, brought home from the west coast from this time on, were to be totally absorbed into the Portuguese race.

Traffic with the west coast of Africa continued to increase. In 1445 four separate expeditions, a total of twenty-six ships, sailed from Portugal. These included for the first time a fleet fitted out in Lisbon and a second group from Lagos once more under the command of D. Lançarote. Dinis Fernandes is given the credit for being the first to reach Cape Verde and both he and D. Lançarote entered the estuary of the Senegal which lies to the north of the Cape. They found that this river, which the Portuguese called Çanaga and the natives Ouedech, was the boundary between the Azanegues and the Jalofes. To the north the people were mostly of Moorish descent, to the south they were negroes. Though perhaps at first they hardly realized it, the Portuguese had left the desert behind and would soon reach the forest country, they had passed the northern boundaries of Guinea proper.

Before they left for the south, D. Henrique's captains were given strict instructions to establish friendly relations with the tribesmen they met and not to involve themselves in warlike adventures. One can see the hand of the Regent in this, for he was determined to do what he could to encourage exploration and legitimate trade. But the captains often did not view their activities in this light; even allowing for the lack of a common language and the misunderstandings to which this gave rise, it is clear that, once they were on their own, they only too often flatly disobeyed their orders. In building up their vast overseas empire, the Portuguese showed on countless occasions almost superhuman courage and endurance: they won victories against astonishing odds; individuals sometimes achieved notable successes by peaceful means. But all this was too often marred by cruelty, jealousy, intolerance, greed and indiscipline. This was perhaps their greatest failing; leaders disobeyed the orders of the Government, captains left the fleet to sail away on private excursions of their own, crews refused to obey their officers.

It was inevitable that some captains should prefer a quick raid on the coast in search of slaves to edging in and out of muddy and unhealthy estuaries in the interests of geography. But the unctuous approval with which Azurara records these slave raids leaves an unpleasant taste. For example, members of the 1445 expedition from Lisbon made a series of attacks on the fishing villages on the island of Tider and the neighbouring coast. ' "By the grace of God," ' says their leader, ' "I shall take you to the place where the Moors are and, if we can find them, the booty cannot but be good . . . Wherefore I call upon you to remember your honour and act bravely. And now let us go on our way, for God will be with us. . . ." The enemy, finding themselves surrounded, pinned all their hopes in flight. But the Portuguese captured forty-six of them besides those who were killed at the first impact. . . . The captain then told his comrades of his joyful victory. . . . The Moors did not wait to count the number of their enemies, but fled in terror. But this served them little, for only two escaped; three were killed and seven taken. . . . But what troubled them most after the trials of the night was to find in the village nothing of what they sought. . . . The Moors not only lacked courage to defend themselves, but even the will to escape. And our men took in all ten of them, including men, women and children. . . . Let each man now run as fast as he can and fall upon them bravely. But if we are not able to make captives of the young men, let us seize the old men, the women and the children. And whoever defends himself, let him be slain without pity. . . . In all there were taken captive thirty-five Moors besides some that perished. And the captain received great praise for his deeds. . . . The Moors sought mercy and this they were granted, for if they had been killed, the profit would not have been so great. . . .'

Towards the end of his book, Azurara calculates that by 1448, 927 captives in all had been brought back to Portugal.

D. Henrique, or perhaps it was D. Pedro, was not altogether satisfied with exploring the coast and relying on hearsay for the secrets of the interior. It was greatly to their satisfaction, therefore, when João Fernandes offered to go on shore near the Rio de Ouro and live on the country until he could be picked up in the following year. He was one of the first of that intrepid band of Portuguese travellers who, during the next century or two, found their way to the remotest parts of Asia, Africa and South America, often to places which no European was to see again until the nineteenth century. Adaptable and self-reliant, they cheerfully faced the hazards and discomforts of the African bush. Many lost their lives in unrecorded tragedies, falling victims to hunger, thirst or exhaustion, to fever or snake-bite, to the poisonous brew of a witch-doctor or a jealous husband, to the thrust of a spear in the deep forest or to the fury of a river in flood. Some came safely home to tell the story of their adventures to the King, but their accounts lay buried in the archives until they were destroyed in the Lisbon earthquake of 1755: now even their names are forgotten. A few wrote descriptions of their journeys or caught the interest of the chroniclers.

João Fernandes was one of the lucky ones who survived and indeed at a later date his experiences would not have been especially noteworthy. He was better equipped than some, for he spoke Arabic fluently: he had learnt it the hard way—in an Moorish prison. He was well treated by the group of Tuareg whom he fell in with soon after he landed. True, they stripped him of his clothes, but in exchange they gave him a robe such as they wore themselves; they robbed him of the biscuits and wheat flour he had brought with him and ate them on the spot, but they fed him on their own dried fish and raw meat and the milk and cheese they lived on in the desert.

After some weeks two messengers on camels arrived to invite him to visit their master, Chief Ahude Meynon, who lived some way off in the interior. 'This would please me well', said Fernandes, 'for I hear he is a noble Lord and I would much like to meet him.'

The journey across the desert was not without incident, for at one time Fernandes and his escort had to go three days without water. But in the end they arrived safely to be greeted by an old gentleman who looked and lived like an Old Testament prophet. Fernandes spent several months with the Chief and no doubt he made good use of his time to learn all he could about the people, the geography and the trade of the country. When the time came for him to return to the coast, his host paid him the compliment of going with him. But his relief must have been great when the sails of a caravel appeared over the horizon and he knew that he had not been forgotten.

Fernandes must have reported to the Infante by word of mouth. What he said is summarized by Azurara in a few lines. 'The heat is very great and so is the dust from the sand. Most of the people travel on foot, but a few on horse-back and others on camels. Though the grazing is scanty, there are great numbers of camels of all colours. The men of rank own captive negroes and possess much gold, which they bring from the land of the negroes. There are in that land many ostriches and deer, gazelles, partridges and hares. Swallows which depart from Portugal in the summer come to this land of sand, but the storks pass over to winter in the land of the negroes.'

Sooner or later the activities of the slave raiders were bound to end in tragedy. Soon after D. Lançarote had returned from his first voyage, D. Henrique fitted out another caravel and gave the command to Gonçalo de Sintra, a young man of his household in whom he had the greatest confidence. The captain's orders were to explore beyond Cape Verde, but instead he disembarked on the island of Tartaraguas, in the Arguim archipelago, to look for slaves. But by this time the islanders were beginning to know what was in store for them when the caravels appeared and fled into the bush. Gonçalo found nothing but deserted villages. Unwisely he continued his search through the night. In the morning he found that the tide had risen and his boat lay on the far side of a wide lagoon. As he approached by the head of the lagoon, the rocks around them, which had seemed to be deserted, were suddenly alive with armed men. Five of the Portuguese swam to safety across the inlet, but Gonçalo himself, who could not swim, and six of his companions, lost their lives in the ambush.

In the following year there was another disaster in which Nuno Tristão and most of his crew were killed. This captain was one of the Infante's most loyal servants, a dedicated explorer, who, it will be remembered, had been entrusted with the first caravel. He was not a man to disobey orders and his voyage in 1446 took him to the furthest point yet reached, beyond the mouth of the Gambia, a river so large that the water was fresh two leagues out to sea which must, they thought, be the long-sought western branch of the Nile. Sixty leagues beyond Cape Verde, Nuno came on yet another unknown river which flowed into a broad estuary through thick, mysterious forests. He launched the ship's boats and followed the winding river inland. His men found it fascinating and beautiful. But suddenly their enjoyment was cut short by a shower of arrows, smeared with a poison so deadly that four of them died before they could reach the ship. With great difficulty the survivors climbed on board, hauled up the anchor and set the sails and then, one by one, they died. Only the captain's clerk, a youth called Aires Tinoco, two young pages, a half-breed slave and a servant, were un-harmed. Only two of the wounded, after weeks of illness, threw off the effects of the poison. The bodies of Nuno Tristão and eighteen of his men were buried at sea.

It is not, perhaps, surprising that the return of this ship caught the fancy of the chroniclers. Aires Tinoco had no training in seamanship but he had been brought up in sur-roundings where such matters were common talk and had no doubt listened while his elders discussed their problems. He was able not only to set a course for home, but also, because a caravel was light and easily handled, to keep it, with the help of his makeshift crew, more or less on the course he had laid down. At long last they fell in with another vessel, not a Moor, as they had feared, but a Galician corsair belonging to one Pero Falcão. He told them, to their great relief, that they were not far from the coast of Portugal, in the latitude of Sines, and offered to guide them to Lagos.

It is worth noting that a caravel, the sort of ship in which the Portuguese undertook these expeditions into unknown waters, tiny cockleshells of fifty tons or thereabouts, could be handled by three men and two boys and, even when fully manned, often carried a crew of less than thirty.

In 1447 yet another tragedy occurred. The victim this time was a Danish knight called Abelhart, who had come to Portugal to offer his services to the Infante. It so hap-pened that the Portuguese were about to send an embassy to Africa to visit a powerful monarch who was supposed, from his capital in the interior, to rule over all the peoples in the neighbourhood of Cape Verde. They were as yet unfamiliar with the African tribal system and still took it for granted that they would encounter kings and kingdoms in the European pattern. It may be that the stories they had heard referred to the Fulani federation of Tekrar, which lay between the Jalofos (Waloffs) on the coast and the kingdoms of Mali and Songhor on the Niger. The Fulani were the descendants of the first wave of Arab invaders who had crossed the Sahara several centuries before. They were staunch Muslims, but it seems that D. Henrique was convinced that their ruler was a Christian. If this were so, he would certainly be a valuable ally against the Moors and might even prove to be the legendary Prester John himself. Who better then than this tall, blonde Dane to accompany Fernão Afonso, the official ambassador, and add distinction to his retinue?

Barros tells the tale of the unfortunate incident which led to the death of Abelhart. 'At first the natives were suspicious', he says, 'but when they learnt that the ship had brought an embassy and gifts for their king, they became less hostile and agreed to send a message to him, for he was engaged on a raid some eight days journey away inland. Meanwhile hostages were exchanged and one and all began to bring goods for trade. Among the things the negroes brought were the tusks of elephants which pleased Balarte [Abelhart] very much. He asked if they could show him a live elephant and if not, if they could bring him the skin and bones of one, promising a big prize to him who could show what he wanted. And after three days they came back to call Balarte, saying that the elephant was now ready for him to see.

'Balarte set out for the shore in the ship's boat, accompanied only by the oarsmen. When they had reached the shore, one of the negroes handed a sailor a gourd of palm-wine and he leant so far over the side of the boat to reach it that he fell into the water. In their haste to save him, his companions forgot about the boat which floated away and was carried a little way out to sea by the swell. When the negroes saw that our party was unarmed and could not be helped from the ship, they fell upon them and none of them escaped, save one who knew how to swim and who brought back news of the affair. As he swam, he looked back and saw Balarte standing in the bow of the boat and defending himself from the attacks of his enemies. In such a manner', ends Barros, 'perished this good man who sought honour outside his own country, but who met his death in Guinea, so far and so different from his native Denmark.'

The last voyage recorded by Azurara was more successful. In 1448, he tells us, Álvaro Fernandes reached a point 110 leagues beyond Cape Verde, an exploit which would have taken him to the neighbourhood of the modern town of Kanakry. This was, as it turned out, the most southerly landfall reached during the lifetime of D. Henrique. Fernandes also, according to Barros, made use of an antidote for the arrow poison. In spite of this, the weapons of the forest-dwellers added an additional hazard to the voyages of discovery, since the sailors could not even be certain of filling their water casks in safety. It was also becoming clear that although a river such as the Senegal or the Gambia was sometimes referred to as an 'Earthly Paradise', the country was quite exceptionally unhealthy. Tropical diseases are not often mentioned by the chroniclers, but malaria, typhoid and dysentery must often have taken their toll.

It may have been partly for these reasons that in 1448 or thereabouts the Portuguese decided to build a fort on the island of Arguim. Both for traders and explorers a foreward base was necessary where fresh water could readily be obtained; where the sick and wounded could be looked after in greater comfort than in the cramped quarters of a caravel; where the fishing fleets which had begun to visit these parts in growing numbers could seek protection and to which, it was hoped, an increasing share in the Moors' Saharan trade could be diverted.

During the Regency D. Henrique had begun to build himself a new headquarters on the boulder-strewn promontory at Sagres. Both the purpose and the exact site of his *Vila* there have been hotly debated. He himself referred to it as 'my *Vila* at Sagres', or 'my *Vila* at Terçanable', a name that has been variously derived. It has been argued that it was connected with the word 'arsenal', itself of Arabic origin, because it was here that the expeditions to Guinea were fitted out. But it has also been derived from *Tarf Anabel*, the Cape of Hannibal, said to be the name given to the locality by the Carthaginians. There were—and are—two capes at Sagres: the more westerly, three miles across the bay from Cape St. Vincent, is now known as the *Ponta de Sagres*, and the second, a mile further east, is called *Ponta da Atalaia*. Between them lies the *Praia da Moreta* ('the Beach of the Small Waves') which, in spite of its name, is only partially sheltered from the south-west. But, tucked away round the corner of the *Ponta da Atalaia* is a second bay facing east and sheltered both from the north and the west. In this anchorage the local fishermen moor their boats to this day; here, no doubt, fifteenth-century sailors would have put in for shelter if the weather was unsuitable for doubling Cape St. Vincent, and here would have been the scene of any experiments in ship-building which might have been carried out at Sagres. Some substantial ruins overlook this anchorage and it has been claimed that these are the remains of the *Vila do Infante*.

Nevertheless, it seems reasonably certain that the *Vila* was in fact built on the more westerly of the two promontories,

within the walls of the old Moorish fort. This is the traditional site where the chapel, attributed to D. Henrique,
still stands. In a letter written shortly before his death,
the Infante himself stated that his *Vila* was on the first of
the two capes reached by those travelling from west to
east. When Drake sacked the town in 1587, one of his
officers drew a sketch-map (now in the British Museum)
which shows the buildings within the confines of the old
fort[4].

D. Henrique is said to have established at Sagres an
academy for the study of navigation, geography, astronomy
and other kindred subjects. A monument, a copy of one of
the pillars set up by Diogo Cão on the coast of Africa, has
recently been erected at Sagres to commemorate these
activities. But there is no evidence that in the literal sense
any such academy ever existed. The town, it seems, was
only the headquarters of a School of Navigation in the
sense that Athens was the seat of a School of Philosophy.
In addition to the chapel, the sketch-map of 1587 shows
two small houses, a defensive tower, a retaining wall and
a two-storey block of what appear to be single rooms or
cells. Parts of these buildings can still be seen, the rest are
said to have been destroyed in an earthquake.

Sagres, then, was the last anchorage before Cape St.
Vincent for shipping heading for the Atlantic, Lisbon,
Gascony, England or Flanders. In the winter months storms
blow up from the south-west and throughout the year
there are times when the wind sets steadily from the north.
In these conditions neither sailing ships nor galleys could
safely weather the Cape and they would then have put into
Sagres to await a change in the wind. As the news of the
Portuguese discoveries spread over Europe, sailors, pas-
sengers and merchants such as Cadamosto, weather-bound
in the bay, would have sought out the architect of these

discoveries with whom they could be certain of an interesting and stimulating discussion. The farm at Raposeira, some miles away over a bleak and windy plateau, was inconvenient and much too small to accommodate all these visitors, and the Infante had to find room for them at Sagres.

To a man so interested in ships and the sea as D. Henrique, the view from the promontory would have been endlessly exhilarating, with the ocean on three sides, the bluff headland of Cape St. Vincent to the west, and, even on the calmest days, the growl of the waves breaking in the caverns at the foot of the cliffs. But the tradition of the 'Hermit of Sagres' cannot be supported by the facts. Although, as he grew older, the Infante spent more and more time in the Algarve, it is clear from his correspondence that, even when he was there, he was constantly concerned with the management of his own estates, with the affairs of the Order of Christ and with new ways of raising money to cover the expenses of his ventures. In addition, he paid frequent visits to the Court, at Setúbal or Santarém, or wherever it happened to be, and spent a good deal of time at the headquarters of his Order at Tomar.

6

The Last Years of Henry the Navigator

During the Regency, D. Pedro's influence was just as great at home as it was overseas. The University of Coimbra, which is one of the oldest in Europe, owed its charter to him, but he was chiefly occupied with the completion of the body of law known as the *Ordinações Afonsinas*. This great task had been begun by João I, continued under D. Duarte and finally completed by Rui Fernandes in 1446. It covered both civil and criminal law and included sections on taxation and the fiscal system and the rights and privileges of the Church. It replaced a tangle of royal edicts, enactments by the Cortes and local, feudal and ecclesiastical charters, customs and privileges. By gathering the threads of justice firmly into the hands of the King, it offered a hope of fair dealing to the people and deprived the nobility and, to a lesser extent, the Church of many of their ancient prerogatives.

The *Ordinances* did not make the Regent any more popular with the Duke of Bragança who was still nursing his grievances on his estates in northern Portugal. Although the Duke was now a man of seventy, his jealousy of his step-brother and his resentment at the way life had treated him only seemed to grow with the years. His grudges were shared by his elder son, the Count of Ourém, who had joined his father in self-imposed exile from the Court when the Regent had refused to appoint him to the office of Constable.

As long as Afonso V was still a minor, the Duke and his partisans were powerless. But by Portuguese law the King came of age when he was fourteen and when this happened, in January 1446, the conspirators set to work to undermine D. Pedro's position. They were disappointed to find that at first nothing was changed, for the King showed his gratitude to his ex-tutor and Regent by asking him to remain in office until he felt more sure of himself. He was much looking forward to his marriage to his cousin Isabel, the daughter of D. Pedro, who had been his constant companion throughout his childhood and with whom he was now deeply in love.

This state of affairs did not suit the Braganças at all. They were, however, greatly assisted by the Archbishop of Lisbon, who made use of his privileged position to approach the King in private and suggest to him that it was time he cut himself free from the apron-strings of his uncle and stood on his own feet. Afonso V is usually called 'O *Africano*', because of his victories in North Africa. But he might more suitably have been called 'Afonso the Erratic'. He was unstable and often irresponsible and, as will be seen, was to plunge his country into near-disaster from which he had to be rescued by his son. At the age of fourteen he was both credulous and naive, perfect material for intrigue. The Braganças and their cronies had no difficulty in persuading him to believe the worst about D. Pedro. They reminded him how his uncle had torn him from the arms of his mother when he was still a child of only six years old and how his mother had soon afterwards died in mysterious circumstances. They suggested that the deaths of his father D. Duarte and his younger uncle, D. João, had also never been satisfactorily explained. They told him that the office of Constable, which the Regent had given to his own son, belonged by rights to the Count

*Prince Henry the Navigator (centre, right). The kneeling
figure in the foreground is said to be the future King João II*

Henry the Navigator's chapel at Sagres

Model of a caravel

of Ourém. It was not long before the King decided that he could, after all, manage on his own.

D. Pedro was not by nature an intriguer and he was caught unprepared by Afonso's ingratitude and by the sudden wave of unpopularity which surrounded him. Perhaps mistakenly, he asked permission to withdraw to Coimbra, where, he said, his estates needed attention. The Braganças, having once separated uncle and nephew, were determined to keep them apart. D. Henrique, hurrying up from Sagres to plead for his brother, found himself cold-shouldered by the King. The Queen who, if she had been a little older, might have intervened successfully on her father's behalf, was bewildered and terrified by what was happening. Even the people of Lisbon who, a few years before, had wanted to put up a statue of the Regent, began to desert their former hero. By 1449 D. Pedro could only rely on his own retainers and that old war-horse, D. Álvaro Vaz de Almada, Count of Avranches and Knight of the Garter, who had returned from a campaign in Ceuta to be at his old friend's side.

At this point the Count of Ourém, who seems to have been the brains of the conspiracy, suggested to his father that he should move to Santarém, where the Court was installed and that, in order to get there, he should lead his armed followers across D. Pedro's lands near Coimbra. This, in the idiom of the time, was a mortal affront, which the Regent determined to resist. He did so successfully in so far as the Duke abjectly turned tail at the sight of him and eventually reached his destination with some difficulty through the melting snows of the Serra de Estrela. But by taking up arms D. Pedro had laid himself open to a charge of treason. The King offered him a choice of prison, exile or death.

Sadly, D. Pedro decided that his only hope lay in meeting

the King himself. With some misgiving, he set out for Santarém, but, hoping to avoid a head-on collision with the King's forces, he edged gradually westward. But the Braganças were not going to let their quarry escape. On 20th May 1449, they came up with him at Alfarrobeira, near the Tagus, a few miles north-east of Lisbon. In the insignificant skirmish which followed, the Prince was killed. His old companion in arms, D. Álvaro Vaz, died with him, fighting to the last.

Throughout these tragic months, D. Henrique, in attendance at the Court, did what he could to find an acceptable compromise. But the impressionable young King was much more ready to listen to the flatteries of the colourful Braganças than to the sensible and moderate suggestions of his other uncle with his subfusc garments and ascetic habits. Those who belittled D. Henrique were afterwards to say that he was more concerned with retaining the grants and privileges he had received during the Regency than with the fate of the Regent himself. At best, with the martyrdom of one brother already on his conscience, he must have wondered miserably whether he had done all he could to save D. Pedro. But of course the Braganças did not want sensible suggestions, they were out for blood and they swept the King along with them.

Records for the period from 1449 to 1455 are scanty, but we know that D. Henrique spent much of this time at Court. In 1451, for instance, he was occupied with the marriage by proxy of his niece Leonor, the daughter of D. Duarte, to the Emperor Frederic III, and the organization of the fleet in which she set out to join her husband. But whether this exile from his beloved Algarve was self-imposed because he had not yet recovered from the shock of his brother's death or at the instance of the King, because the Braganças preferred to have him near at hand where they could keep an eye on him, there is no means of telling. It does not seem that he could have been officially out of favour, for it was during these years that Azurara wrote his *Chronicle* on the King's instructions and this, as has already been shown, is an unreserved tribute to the Infante.

By the time the narrative of Cadamosto opens, however, there had been a clear change of policy in West Africa. The Portuguese were engaged in exploiting the regions they already knew, in filling in the details of their previous discoveries and in colonizing the Atlantic islands. Although captains were still given a general instruction 'to go as far as they could', the exploration of new lands and the search for a sea-way to the Indies for the time being took second place. It was not, in fact, until 1462, two years after the death of D. Henrique, that any further progress southward was made and Pêro de Sintra reached and passed the mountains of Sierra Leone.

It has been suggested that there is a clue to this change of policy in the fierce currents, mentioned both by Cadamosto and by Diogo Gomes, which set to the southward beyond the mouth of the Gambia. But it is much more likely that D. Henrique simply could not afford any longer to fit out expeditions from which he could expect no immediate profit, and that, when the Guinea voyages were resumed, he was working to a plan already shaped during the Regency. The fortified post of Arguim, through which much of the trade of both the Sahara and Guinea was channelled, had probably already been completed by the end of 1448 and occupied by a small permanent garrison of soldiers and officials. This fort was an important prop to the new policy and the decision to build it had certainly been taken before the fall of D. Pedro.

Another new trend was the attempt to attract foreign capital. Individual foreigners had already taken part in several of the earlier voyages, but by 1454 it seems that a regular routine had been established for visiting ships which put into Lagos or Sagres. In that year Cadamosto joined the galleys of the Flanders fleet in Venice and set out for northern Europe.

'Contrary winds', he tells us, 'delayed the galleys at Cape St. Vincent, so that by chance I found myself at no great distance from the place where the Lord Infante Henrique was lodged at a country estate called Raposeira. When he had news of us, he sent one of his secretaries . . . with samples of sugar from Madeira, dragons' blood and other products of his domains and islands. These he displayed in my presence to many on the galleys. His Lord, he said, had peopled newly-discovered islands previously uninhabited and caused seas to be navigated which had never been sailed. He had discovered the lands of many strange races, where marvels abounded. Those who had been in these parts had wrought great gain among these new peoples, turning one *soldo* into six or ten.'

Cadamosto was told that, under certain conditions, any merchant who wished could take part in these ventures. If the merchant provided both ship and cargo, he must, on his return, pay D. Henrique a quarter of all he brought back. If the Infante provided the caravel, but the merchant supplied the cargo, all that he brought back would be halved. If, by any chance, nothing was brought back, D. Henrique would bear the expenses. There was no argument about the Infante's right to lay down these conditions. From the first a Portuguese captain had required a licence from D. Henrique to sail beyond Cape Bojador. In January 1454, the very year in which Cadamosto came to Sagres, Pope Nicholas V recognized the claims of Afonso V to all newly-discovered lands on or near the west coast of Africa and forbade all Christians to visit them without the permission of the King of Portugal[1]. In 1456 Calixtus III confirmed these pronouncements and granted to the Order of Christ spiritual jurisdiction over all the 'islands, towns, ports, countries and states, from the Capes of Bojador and Não, throughout all Guinea, and beyond that southern region as far as the Indies'[2].

The Venetian Cadamosto was not the only foreigner to invest in the Guinea trade during the last years of D. Henrique's life, for he was to fall in with a caravel commanded by Antoniotto Usodimare, while during the same period we hear of the exploits of Antonio da Noli, who claimed to be the discoverer of the Cape Verde Islands. Both these captains were Genoese.

The desire to attract foreign capital may also have been the cause of an incident which took place in 1459. In that year a Conference was held at Florence. It was attended by certain Florentine merchants, by envoys of the King of Portugal and by the famous geographer, Toscanelli. It may be that Afonso V, or perhaps D. Henrique, hoped to ally Portuguese expertise with Florentine money and that the Florentines had called in Toscanelli to advise them. Nothing came of this project. It must be supposed that Toscanelli, whose ideas are said to have inspired Columbus, was already convinced that the Indies could more easily be reached by sailing to the west than by persevering with the attempt to find a way round southern Africa and that he so advised the men of Florence. One thing is abundantly clear, however; that whatever may have been the policy of the Portuguese in earlier years, or later on during the reign of João II, at this time they saw no reason to keep their activities secret.

It was from the Conference at Florence, apparently, that

Fernão Martins brought back to Portugal the map of Fra Mauro, previously commissioned in Venice by Afonso V. If this map was one of the working papers of the Conference, it must have been studied with very great interest, for it was a considerable advance on anything which had been produced before. It drew on the journeys of Marco Polo and the more recent experiences of Nicola da Conti for details of the continent of Asia. Contrary to the views of the Ptolemeans, it showed the Indian Ocean to be an open sea; it included much accurate information of Arabic origin about the east coast of Africa, although the large island of Diab, situated off the southern extremity of the continent, proved to have no existence in fact; it showed a deep gulf, cut deep into the heart of Africa at the approximate latitude of the Gulf of Guinea. But the waterways of Africa still defeated the cartographers. Fra Mauro depicted a branch of the Nile flowing westward to enter the Atlantic through the mouths of the Senegal and the Gambia.

The narratives of Cadomosto and Diogo Gomes cover the last six years of D. Henrique's life. According to his account, which he wrote some years later, after his return to Venice, Cadamosto took part in two expeditions, the first in 1455 and the second in the following year. Gomes also made two voyages to Guinea: the stories of his first voyage and of Cadamosto's second have so much in common that it has been suggested that they travelled in company, but since neither captain mentions the other, this cannot be proved.

Apart from his claim that he, rather than da Noli, was the first to sight the Cape Verde Islands, Cadamosto made no new discoveries. But his narrative is in many ways more interesting than the *Chronicles* of Azurara. He was a private citizen, not an official historian with a special responsibility for the prestige of his master. He was a merchant from a city of merchants and his survey of West African trade remained a standard work for many years. He was deeply interested in everything he saw and heard and his book is full of details about the customs and way of life both of the Azanegues who dwelt in the desert and the negroes who lived by the Senegal and Gambia. Above all, he was the first person to record his experiences who had actually visited West Africa. He did not, therefore, try to interpret the new lands in terms of Europe. He understood, for instance, as Azurara did not, the African system of tribes and chiefs. He realized how fundamentally different was the life of the tribesmen from that to which his fellow Europeans were accustomed and he could see for himself how poor the people were and how limited was their outlook.

Cadamosto had a very clear picture of the trade routes of the Sahara. No doubt much of what he tells us was already known in Portugal, from explorers like João Fernandes and the merchants at Arguim, but, if so, the records have not survived. 'You should know', he writes, 'that the Lord Infante of Portugal has leased the island of Arguim to Christians, so that no one may enter the bay to trade with the Arabs save those who hold a licence. They have dwellings on the island and "factories" where they buy and sell with the said Arabs who come to the coast to trade for merchandise of various kinds, such as cotton or woollen cloth, cloaks, carpets and, above all, corn, for they are always short of food. They give in exchange slaves, whom they bring from the land of the Blacks, and gold dust.

'You should also know that about six days journey inland by camel there is a place called Woden. It is not walled, but is frequented by Arabs and is a market where caravans arrive from Tanbutu [Timbuktu] and other places in the land of the Blacks, on the way to our nearer Barbary. The food of these people is dates and barley; they drink the milk of camels and other animals, for they have no wine. They are Mohammedans and very hostile to Christians. They never remain settled, but are always wandering over the desert. They have many camels on which they carry brass wire and silver from Barbary to Tanbutu, and from thence they carry away gold and pepper. They also have many Berber horses, which they exchange for slaves, ten or fifteen slaves being given for one of these horses, according to their quality. The Arabs likewise take articles of Moorish silk, made in Granada or Tunis or Barbary, silver and other goods, obtaining in exchange any number of slaves and some gold.

'Beyond the mart of Woden, six days further inland, is a place called Taghaza, where a great quantity of rock salt is mined. Every year large caravans of camels carry it to Tanbutu; from there they go to Mali, the Empire of the Blacks, and there it is sold at two to three hundred ducats a load.'

Cadamosto goes on to explain how the salt is then sold in Wagara for gold through the 'silent trade' and has to be carried there on the heads of porters. From Mali the gold is distributed in all directions. Some goes to Cairo by way of Gao and the eastern oases; some across the central Sahara to Tunis and some by way of Woden to the ports of north-west Africa. Of this last share, the Portuguese in Arguim were able to buy a very small part.

Later in the century, the Portuguese were to open a trading post at Woden in an attempt to tap the Sahara trade direct, but this venture was not successful and the post was soon abandoned. It should be noted that the peppers to which Cadamosto refers are chillies, also called *malagueta* or 'grains of paradise'. Chillies from West Africa were never so popular as black pepper from the Indies; when the

Portuguese finally reached India and the Spice Islands, the market for *malagueta* dwindled away.

Cadamosto was the first to distinguish clearly between the northern 'Arabs' and the Azaneghi, the Sanhaja Tuareg who inhabited the country from Cabo Branco to the Senegal river. 'The Arabs', he says, 'are brown complexioned, and wear white cloaks edged with a red stripe: the women also dress in the same way. On their heads the men wear turbans in the Moorish fashion and always go barefooted.' He was also, curiously enough, the first to mention the veil worn by the Tuareg. 'They are dark brown rather than light and always wear a cloth on the head with a flap, which they fold across the face, covering the mouth and part of the nose. They are a very poor people, liars, the biggest thieves in the world and exceedingly treacherous. They wear their hair in locks down to the shoulders and anoint it every day with fish oil, so that it smells strongly and this they consider a great refinement.'

Most of the first slaves brought to Portugal were from the fishing communities of this tribe. But by 1455 D. Henrique had forbidden slave raids on this part of the coast. He hoped that the Azanegues, by trading peacefully with his captains, might be converted to Christianity. Nevertheless, we are told that by this time the Portuguese were carrying away from Arguim a thousand slaves a year. If this figure is correct, it shows how rapidly this trade was increasing, for Azurara's estimate for the total haul up to 1448 is less than that for a single year at the time of Cadamosto's voyage in 1455.

Though some merchants made handsome profits, the Land of Guinea, now that the Portuguese had reached it, was something of a disappointment. It did not seem that Moorish influence had been much disturbed and though most of the negroes who had been brought back to Portugal had readily embraced the Christian faith, there were no signs of any conversions on a large scale in their home-lands. From time to time a few grains of gold dust or a golden ornament or two were greedily snapped up, but they did not seem to be much nearer to the district where the gold was mined. Although ivory was becoming a profitable investment, slaves were still much the most valuable merchandise. North of the Senegal, slaves were most often bartered for horses: five or six slaves, and some-times more, could be exchanged for a horse of little worth. Gomes complains that the market was being ruined: 'Whereas', he says, 'the Moors used to give seven negroes for a horse, now they give no more than six!'

Further south, the articles which the Portuguese could barter were more varied: red and blue cloth, green and yellow beads (made in the Kingdom of Fez especially for the Saharan trade), kerchiefs, brass rings, and wire, basins of the kind used by barbers, bloodstones, tin, coral and a kind of scarlet beret which was to prove popular from one end of Africa to the other. But in addition to the official trade, one can imagine the crew, like sailors the world over, chaffering for ornaments, household utensils, poison-ed arrows and anything else that took their fancy and offering in exchange the *bugigangas*, trifles which they had picked up in the market-places of Portugal.

Budomel, who lived on the southern bank of the Senegal, was a friendly chief and Cadamosto spent some days in his company. The Venetian was not concerned only with marvels and curiosities, but with the details of everyday existence. Anyone who has lived in the remoter parts of Africa will recognize a way of life which has remained almost unchanged until the twentieth century. 'Chief Budomel's people', he tells us, 'wear nothing on their heads; the hair of both sexes, which by nature is no more than a span in length, is arranged in patterns of various styles. The men and women are clean in their persons, since they wash themselves all over four or five times a day. They eat, ten or twelve of them together, all helping themselves from a dish placed in their midst. They are talkative and never at a loss for something to say. They sow and harvest their crops within a space of three months. They are very bad labourers, unwilling to sow more than will barely support themselves for the rest of the year. They hold markets once or twice in the week which both men and women attend from a distance of four or five miles. They bring to the market a little cotton, cotton thread and cloth, vegetables, oil and millet, wooden bowls, palm-leaf mats and all the other articles they use in their daily life. The women spin the cloth a span in width; when they wish to make a larger piece, they join four or five of these strips together. They have only two kinds of musical instruments, drums and a kind of two-stringed lyre, played with the fingers.'

To Cadamosto, Budomel's kingdom was of little account. 'He is Lord only of this part of Senegal and rules over nothing save villages of grass huts. Yet he is treated with the greatest respect. Such lords as he, when granting an audience, display much ceremony. However high-born be he who seeks audience, on entering the door of Budomel's courtyard, he throws himself on his knees, bows his head to the ground, and with both hands scatters dust on his naked shoulders and head. No man would be bold enough to come before him, unless he had stripped himself naked save for his girdle of leather. When within two paces, he begins to relate his business, without ceasing to pour dust on his head.'

As for Cadamosto himself, the people marvelled at his clothing no less than at his white skin. They examined his doublet and the woollen cloth he wore with amazement. Some touched his hands and limbs and rubbed him with spittle to discover whether his whiteness was dye or flesh.

The inhabitants of this part of the coast were Jalofos. Duarte Pacheco, writing fifty years later, said of them, 'Most of these people go naked, except the men of quality who wear shirts of blue cotton cloth and drawers of the same material. All these people, like the Mandingo and Turcorol, are circumcised and worship in the faith of Mafoma. They are vicious, never at peace with one another, great thieves and such liars that they never speak the truth. They are great drunkards and ingrates, so that, although one may do good by them, they are never grateful. They are shameless in asking a higher price for what they have to sell.'

Off the mouth of the Senegal, Cadamosto fell in with two more caravels, one of which was commanded by the Genoese, Usodimare. They decided to join forces. Beyond Cape Verde, they came first to a region of mangrove swamps, which they thought very beautiful. This was the country of the Barbacenes, thickly forested and crossed only by narrow tracks where the tribesmen greeted all strangers with showers of poisoned arrows. Here they made no attempt to land, but at the mouth of a river further to the south, they sent one of their African interpreters ashore to try to make contact with the inhabitants. As they watched, this unfortunate man was cut down and killed.

The river Gambia had been discovered by Nuno Tristão on his last voyage in 1446, but it had never been explored. Cadamosto and his companions made two attempts to enter the river, feeling their way carefully over the shoals at its mouth. But on both occasions they were attacked by war canoes, each manned by thirty warriors or more. On

the second day they became involved in a brisk skirmish
with a fleet of seventeen of these canoes and had to fight
them off with crossbows and bombards.

'They row standing up,' says Cadamosto, 'so many on
each side. They have one man extra in the stern who paddles
now on one side, now on the other, to keep the boat
straight. They do not use thole-pins, but hold the oars
steady in their hands. The oars have a shaft like a short
lance, a yard and a half in length. To the end of this shaft
they bind a round disc and in this manner they paddle
their boats exceedingly swiftly.'

In the end the sailors managed to parley with the Gam-
bians through an interpreter. 'Why', they asked. 'have you
greeted us in this unfriendly way? For we are men of peace
and seek only to trade with you.'

'We have heard of your visit to the Senegal', they
answered, 'and we know that you Christians eat human
flesh and buy black men only to make a meal of them. We
do not want peace on any terms. We hope only to make
an end of you and give all you possess to our Chief.'

In 1456 Cadamosto headed straight for the Gambia. He
was accompanied by Usodimare and by a third caravel
provided by D. Henrique. It must be supposed that
foreigners were not allowed to visit the west coast without
a trustworthy Portuguese to keep an eye on them. On this
occasion, the war canoes left them alone and they were
able to visit a chief called Batimansa, who lived about sixty
miles upstream. Many of the chiefs in this part of Africa
used the Mandingo title *Mansa*, although their empire of
Mali was long past its zenith and in a few years' time even
Timbuktu would fall to the onslaughts of Sonni Ali II of
Songhor.

Cadamosto dismisses the trade of the Gambia in a few
lines: 'Cotton cloth and thread,' we are told, 'sometimes

a gold ring or two, baboons and apes; sometimes the musk of a civet cat, a valuable base for perfume, could be exchanged for a few trifles of little worth.' He devotes more space to a description of the baobab tree and the patterns which the women tattooed on their necks, arms and breasts. He is even more interested in the elephants and the methods used for hunting them. He thought the flesh tasteless, but announces proudly that he was the first of his countrymen to try it. He brought home the foot of an elephant, a portion of its trunk and some of its hairs and presented them to D. Henrique.

Diogo Gomes has more to say about the Gambia. His first voyage probably took place in 1457. According to his narrative, as recalled by Martin Behaim, he went first to the far south and was able to obtain there cotton cloth, ivory and a small quantity of *malagueta* pepper. But the strong currents in the estuary of a river he calls the Fancaso forced him to turn back; his fellow-captains believed that they had reached the utmost limits of the ocean.

Gomes claims to have ascended the Gambia as far as the important market town of Cantor, one hundred and fifty miles from its mouth. Here he met traders from as far afield as Timbuktu and Gao, the capital of the rising empire of Songhor. These traders told him of the great King 'Bormelli' in whose country there was an abundance of gold; outside his palace was to be seen a nugget so large that it took twenty men to move it and to which the King used to tie his horse. They told him also of the range of mountains called the Futa Jallon, the watershed which divided the westward-flowing rivers such as the Senegal and Gambia from the 'river of Emin' and its tributaries which flowed to the east. The existence of these mountains, though neither Gomes nor Behaim, nor for that matter anyone else in Europe, seemed to realize it, was convincing proof that the Niger flowed from west to east and could not therefore be a branch of the Nile on its way to discharge its waters into the Atlantic.

Yet, even in the time of Duarte Pacheco, writing at the beginning of the sixteenth century, most Portuguese still thought that the Senegal and the Gambia were branches of the Nile. In his *Esmeraldo*, Pacheco writes, 'The source of this river [the Senegal] is unknown to the people who live on it, but we know that it flows from a great lake on the Nile which is some thirty leagues long and ten leagues wide. It appears that this branch flows across Ethiopia Inferior towards the west. At the head of the lake is the kingdom of Tumbuku and there is the great city of the same name at the lake side. Not far off is the town of Jani, surrounded by walls of mud, populated by negroes and with a great wealth of gold. Its markets are full of brass and copper, blue and red cloth, salt, cloves, pepper, saffron, silk and sugar.'

The lake to which Duarte Pacheco refers is presumably the flooded area of the middle Niger and it has been suggested that the town of Jani (or Jinné) is the origin of the name 'Guinea', which came to be applied to the whole region.

'In the river Gambia', continues Pacheco, 'there are many sea horses, of all the colours which horses on land are wont to be. They have the body of an ox, but they have the head and the neck, the hair and the ears of a horse. They have two small horns, as thick as a man's arm at the wrist, and two palms in length. They live in the water, but go out on shore to graze or sleep in the sun. There are also in this river many big lizards, as much as twenty-four feet long from their tails to the tips of their snouts. They also live in the water, but leave it when they wish to lay their eggs, which are bigger than ducks' eggs and which they bury in the sand. They are about a palm's length when they come out of the egg and immediately they seek the nearest river where they finish growing. They are very noxious beasts and they eat men and cows and bullocks.'

To return to Gomes, he was able to make friends with several of the chiefs who lived on the banks of the Gambia, including Batimansa, whom Cadamosto had met, and Numimansa, who was said to have been responsible for the canoe attacks on him. This chief had quite changed his tune and went so far as to ask Gomes to baptize him; this Gomes could not do, as he was not ordained, but he did offer to ask the King to send priests to his country so that the Chief and his people could be instructed in the Faith.

This sequence of voyages was interrupted by the Portuguese expedition to Alcácer-Seguer which took place in the autumn of 1458. The assault on this fortress, which lies on the North African coast between Ceuta and Tangier, was the indirect result of the capture of Constantinople by the Turks in 1453. The fall of this city was not, of course, unexpected, for the Sultan's armies had been threatening it for many years and had already overrun much of south-eastern Europe. But the immediate effect was to cut off from their base in Constantinople the merchant colonies of Venice and Genoa and to disrupt trade in the Black Sea and the ports of northern Asia Minor. In answer to an appeal for help from the Republics on behalf of their colonies the Pope preached a new Crusade.

The monarchs of western Europe made speeches and discussed grandiose plans. Philip the Good of Burgundy declared himself ready to lead the Crusade and held a memorable banquet to celebrate his oath to take the Cross. But times had changed. The Balkans were a long way off.

No one was ready to translate words into deeds, except the King of Portugal. His country was only slowly emerging from its medieval chrysalis and Afonso V was more old-fashioned than most. He at once set about collecting ships and men to form part of a Christian counter-attack in the eastern Mediterranean. D. Henrique sent the Sultan a letter, which was in effect a knightly challenge, and dispatched three copies by different routes to make sure it reached its destination. The King had new gold coins struck, the *cruzados*, which for a century or more were to be acceptable currency all over the world. But when his preparations were far advanced, Afonso discovered that he alone had answered the call and that even the merchant states of Italy, who were most directly threatened by the Turkish success, had made no move.

What, then, was to be done? The Portuguese forces could not hope to challenge the Sultan on their own. So might this not be an opportunity to avenge D. Fernão by a new attack on Tangier? One can see the hand of D. Henrique behind this suggestion. But the King's Council, although they welcomed the idea of a new enterprise in Morocco, were doubtful about Tangier, and chose the lesser fortress of Alcácer-Seguer instead. With this decision D. Henrique had to be content. Although he was sixty-four years old, he threw himself into the preparations with all his old vigour. In October 1458 he set out once more for North Africa; he had himself collected a substantial part of the army of 25,000 men and the fleet of over 200 ships. When the fleet reassembled after its voyage in the Bay of Tangier, the Infante was still eager to attack the city, but wiser counsels, or perhaps it was the faint-heartedness of the King's advisers, prevailed.

At Alcácer-Seguer, D. Henrique, despite his age, was one of the first to disembark. The battle was something of an anticlimax. The Moors fought well, but they were no match for their assailants and D. Henrique himself received the surrender of their leaders. After an absence of little more than a week, the King was back in Portugal with the greater part of his victorious army. The fortress was left in charge of D. Duarte de Meneses, the son of the hero of Ceuta, and it was on his shoulders that most of the fighting fell, for the King of Fez made a strenuous, but unsuccessful attempt to regain the town.

After this short but satisfactory campaign, D. Henrique returned to the Algarve. Since he had both men and ships at hand, he lost no time in resuming the voyages to Guinea. He remembered the promise which Gomes had given to Chief Numimansa and sent out the Abbot of Soto de Casa to instruct him in the Faith. Gomes himself also sailed once more for the south, probably in the spring of 1459, falling in with two other caravels off Cape Verde, one of which was commanded by the Genoese captain, Antonio da Noli.

On this occasion a Spanish interloper named de Prado was captured, sent home to Lisbon and executed by order of the King. On the return voyage, the Cape Verde Islands were visited and the largest of them named Santiago. On reaching Portugal, da Noli, who had had a better homeward passage than Gomes, begged the captaincy of Santiago from the King. Rather surprisingly, since he was a foreigner, and much to the disgust of Gomes, this petition was granted. Cadamosto claimed to have sighted these islands in 1456, when he was blown off course by a storm. He reports that they were uninhabited, clothed with forests which were full of innumerable doves and abounding in turtles and all kinds of fish. There seems no reason to doubt the conclusion that Cadamosto sighted the Cape Verdes when he said he did and made a brief reconnaisance of the most easterly of them, but that they were first explored in detail by da Noli and that Gomes was with him when he did so[3].

These are the last expeditions recorded during the lifetime of D. Henrique. Traditionally his captains reached Sierra Leone before he died, but if they did, no accounts of their exploits have survived. The voyage of Pêro de Sintra, who is credited with the discovery of that region, is assigned to the year 1462 and Cadamosto clearly states that the expedition consisted of two caravels sent thither by the King of Portugal after the death of the Infante. It may be that the discoveries of Sintra were attributed to D. Henrique because the young man was one of his squires; because the Infante was responsible for the preliminary arrangements for the expedition; because it seems to have been the last official voyage based on Lagos, or even because Cadamosto included the story of it in his book with the narrative of his own voyages which took place earlier.

D. Henrique, Infante of Portugal, died peacefully at Sagres on the 13th November 1460 at the age of sixty-seven. He had spent the last few months of his life there, putting his affairs in order. He made his will, for although his expenses had been great, his estates and revenues were still more than considerable. He named as his principal heir his nephew D. Fernão, the King's younger brother, a young man who scarcely seems to have merited his uncle's confidence. He wrote letters inscribed 'at my *Vila*', several of which have survived. In August he granted two of the Açores to D. Fernão[4]; in September he handed over the spiritual jurisdiction of these same islands to the Order of Christ and arranged for masses to be said for his soul[5].

These letters show him to have been in full possession of his faculties almost to the end.

In spite of all the attention which has been lavished on every known detail of his life and work and in spite of all the many thousands of pages which have been written about him, D. Henrique's personality only comes dimly to us over the centuries and he remains to us, as he seems to have been to his contemporaries, an enigma.

7

Afonso the Erratic

From the death of Henry the Navigator in 1460 to the end of the reign of Afonso V in 1481 there was an interlude in the story of the search for a sea-way to the Indies. Although, as will be seen, a good deal of progress was made, neither merchants nor explorers received the support in high places to which they had previously been accustomed.

During this period of twenty years D. Afonso did his best to drag his country back into the fourteenth century. As he grew older it became clear that he had inherited little of the family intelligence and still less of their political flair. Though burly and physically powerful, he remained mentally a jaunty, overgrown adolescent. He liked to think of himself as a knightly king, surrounded by courtiers who served him in the best traditions of chivalry. But as he was totally irresponsible and, moreover, given to wishful thinking, he often found himself embarking on exploits and making promises which all too frequently an unkind fate prevented him from carrying out. Before the bubble burst and he sank in his last years into a mood of self-distrust and dejection, he was able to undo much of what his predecessors had striven to achieve.

His grandfather, D. João I, had always treated with respect the merchants and professional men to whom he owed his throne; he had listened sympathetically to their representatives in the Cortes. Afonso thought nothing of these unknightly fellows who frequently so far forgot themselves as to criticize his government instead of confining themselves to their proper task of providing him with money. It is true that when they grew too refractory he would promise to look into their complaints, but he afterwards conveniently forgot about them. D. João had been generous, some said over-generous, to those of the nobility who supported him, but he was always careful to keep in his own hands enough of the income from the royal estates for his needs. D. Duarte and the Regent had followed his example. But D. Afonso's outlook was purely feudal: he gave away lands and titles without thought for the future. The chief beneficiaries were, of course, the Braganças. The old Duke had died in 1461 and, since his eldest son had died without legitimate heirs in the previous year, Fernão, the second son, succeeded not only to his father's dignities and estates but to those of his brother as well. Although he already rivalled the King in wealth and power, in 1470 he was created Duke of Guimarães.

It is not surprising that neither the King nor his cronies were interested in further voyages of exploration. It required hard, detailed work to fit out a successful expedition to Guinea and, though the results might be profitable, they were not 'honourable'. It was a task better fitted for merchants than for royalty. After his victory at Alcácer-Seguer, D. Afonso's attention was firmly fixed on North Africa, where he could himself take part in knightly deeds against the Moors. Owing more to internal dissensions in Morocco than to the merits of his own generalship, he was surprisingly successful, sufficiently so to earn for himself the by-name of *O Africano*. But he would have been the last to admit the true reasons for his successes, so that, romantic and chivalrous as ever, he then had no hesitation in launching himself into the near-disastrous war of the

Castilian succession in support of his niece Juana. He thus brought to an end the peaceful relations between the two countries which, in spite of many differences, had lasted officially since 1411, and in fact for several years longer.

The King's preoccupation with North Africa did not commend itself to the majority of his subjects, but, given the flimsiest excuse, he was determined to return there. In 1463 he received a message from two Portuguese prisoners in Tangier telling him of the existence of a sewer under the walls through which the city could easily be entered. Without, apparently, taking any steps to verify this story, D. Afonso began at once to prepare for a new assault. It was not his way to keep his plans secret nor to take into account such mundane details as the weather. The campaign was nothing but a series of disasters. The fleet set sail in November: off Lagos it was dispersed by a storm; by the time the battered ships limped one by one into the harbour at Ceuta, the seasick and exhausted troops had been forced to throw most of their equipment overboard. During the next four months, three attacks were made on Tangier. But the Moors were well-prepared and the Portuguese lost several hundred men in attempting to scale the walls; the sewer, if it had ever existed, did not prove a practicable route.

In addition to these setbacks, a raid on Arzila was thwarted by floods and an improvised expedition against the inland hill tribes fell into an ambush. From this last predicament, the King was only extricated by D. Duarte de Meneses, who sacrificed his life in a rear-guard action which allowed his master time to escape. After the battle D. Duarte's body was so badly mutilated by the Moors that his companions could only recover one tooth: this relic can still be seen in the museum at Santarém.

After this last reverse D. Afonso had no choice but to

go home. But he kept in close touch with events in North Africa and when civil war broke out in Morocco, he was quick to seize his chance. The elderly Sultan of Fez, Abdi Alaq, had run into difficulties: his prestige had been greatly lowered by the loss of Alcácer and by his failure to prevent Portuguese depredations in his coastal provinces. He had, moreover, appointed a Jew named Harun to reorganize his finances. Jews were no more popular in Morocco at this time than they were in Spain and Portugal. Consequently the Sultan found himself at odds with the orthodox Muslims, with the 'racists' and with all those whose immunity from taxation seemed likely to be threatened by Harun's reforms. Under the leadership of Sharif Mohammed Aljuti, the rebels seized the capital and the Sultan was deposed and executed; anti-Jewish riots broke out in which Harun and many of his fellow-Jews lost their lives; their property was looted or confiscated.

The Sharif's rule, however, was confined to Fez. Elsewhere he was regarded as an upstart and an usurper. No one resented him more bitterly than Muley Sheikh, a man of noble birth whose father had been Regent during the minority of Abdi Alaq. Muley was at this time Governor of Arzila but he set out at once for Fez with all the troops he could collect. He was forced to lay siege to the city while Arzila was for several months left almost undefended.

D. Afonso had learnt at least some of the lessons of his previous campaign. He sent two merchants to spy out the land; he kept his destination a secret; he chose a more seasonable time of year and he issued detailed plans for the attack. Even so, the expedition almost came to grief. When it arrived off Arzila in late August, a sudden change in the wind forced the King to abandon his prearranged plans for fear of losing his ships on the reefs which guarded the harbour. A precarious landing was made from small boats and two hundred or more soldiers were drowned. Nevertheless, on the first day the Portuguese succeeded in investing the town by land and after four more days of fierce fighting it fell into their hands. The last defenders of the mosque and citadel, who had held out in the hope of help from Mulay Sheikh, were overpowered and massacred; the city was sacked and many of its inhabitants were kille or rounded up to be sold as slaves. Two Portuguese noblemen, the Counts of Marialva and Monsanto, were killed in battle; the young Prince João, who had distinguished himself in the fighting, was knighted by his father on the field.

Meanwhile, Muley Sheikh had raised the siege of Fez to come to the rescue. But when he realized that he was too late, he found himself in a dilemma, for he was now in possession of neither Arzila nor Fez. He decided to make peace with the Portuguese. It was agreed that D. Afonso and his heirs should be Lords of Ceuta, Alcácer-Seguer and Arzila but that they would not oppose the Sheikh's attempt to make himself Sultan of Fez. The treaty contained the curious provision that either party could attack town's surrounded by walls and, with this arrangement, the treaty endured for many years.

These events had an unexpected result. The people of Tangier, hearing that Muley Sheikh had abandoned Arzila, decided to surrender. They feared for their lives and property, for the slaughter and destruction at Arzila had been horrifying. D. João, the son of the Duke of Bragança was sent to take possession of the city and it was occupied without opposition. So the prize which had cost so much heart-burning and cost so many Portuguese lives fell into their laps like an overripe plum.

Among the captives at Arzila had been two of the wives, a son and a daughter of Muley Sheikh. In 1472 they were exchanged for the bones of the Holy Prince, D. Fernão, who had died in prison at Fez nearly thirty years before. In celebration of all these triumphs, D. Afonso took the titles of 'King of Portugal and the Algarves, both on this side and beyond the sea'.

Although neither Afonso V nor his advisers were greatly interested in overseas exploration, more than two thousand miles of unknown coastline were added to the map during the middle years of his reign, a distance far greater than had been discovered in the whole lifetime of D. Henrique[1]. The King had been quick to confirm the terms of his uncle's will. Only a month after the Infante's death, he had granted his brother jurisdiction over Madeira, Porto Santo and the Açores[2]; in 1462 he made a similar grant in respect of the Cape Verde Islands[3]. The letter in which this grant was approved, incidentally, clearly states that five of the islands had been discovered by Antonio da Noli before the death of D. Henrique and the other seven by Diogo Afonso, a squire of the household of D. João himself. These grants were in a standard form, giving to the recipient, his heirs and successors, the islands with all rivers, anchorages, forests, fisheries and coral, together with their mines, vineyards and cattle; rights of all kinds which had previously belonged to the Crown and all jurisdiction civil and criminal, reserving only cases in which the penalty was death or dismemberment.

The voyage of Pêro de Sintra in 1462 has already been briefly mentioned. An account of it is to be found in the last chapter of Cadamosto's book, where the author tells us that it was described to him by a young friend of his who accompanied him on one of his own voyages and who subsequently sailed with de Sintra. It should be noted that

Barros does not mention de Sintra at all but states that one of the two caravels which took part in this expedition was commanded by Soeiro da Costa.

Cadamosto's narrative is brief and factual. It describes and names rivers, promontories, islands and other features over four hundred miles from Cape Varga to Sierra Leone and from there to the neighbourhood of Cape Mesurado, which lies two hundred miles further to the south-east. This south-easterly trend of the coast beyond Sierra Leone was one of the most interesting aspects of de Sintra's discoveries, but at that time no one seems to have drawn any conclusions from it. Cadamosto reports that Serra Leoa, to give it its original Portuguese name, was so called because the thunder growled incessantly among the clouds with which the summits of the mountains were clothed. But Duarte Pacheco, who claims to have spoken to Pêro de Sintra himself, states that it was because of the wild and savage nature of the country and 'for no other reason'.

In 1468 an Italian cartographer called Grazioso Benincasa produced a chart, a copy of which is now in the British Museum, for which he made extensive use, not only of the information gleaned by Cadamosto himself, but also of the descriptions and nomenclature of de Sintra. His was the earliest map to show the Cape Verde Islands.

After de Sintra's return, no further voyages of exploration seem to have taken place for some years. But trade with the Guinea coast continued to flourish and, says Barros, 'The inhabitants became so well-disposed that they came from far in the interior to trade with our people, exchanging merchandise for their fellow-creatures who were brought here more for salvation than for slavery.' The King, however, was too deeply involved in his adventures in North Africa to have much time to spare for other interests and neither he nor his Treasury came in for much share of the profits. Being unwilling to let things run as they were, in 1469 the King granted the request of a Lisbon merchant named Fernão Gomes and farmed out the Guinea trade for a period of five years. In return for a monopoly of the trade, Gomes agreed to pay the King the sum of 200,000 *reis* a year. He undertook also to discover one hundred leagues of coast each year, starting from Serra Leoa. All ivory was to be sold to the King at 1500 *reis* a hundred-weight and Gomes was to be allowed to buy for himself one civet cat each year. Excluded from the agreement was the trade of the coast opposite the Cape Verde Islands which belonged to the Infante D. Fernão and the Arguim trade which had been granted to D. João, the heir to the throne. Shortly afterwards, however, Gomes leased this also for the payment of a further 100,000 *reis* a year. The King reserved to himself the profits on musk, *malagueta* pepper, 'unicorn', spices, precious stones and dyes[4].

As it turned out, Gomes more than fulfilled his part of the agreement. Within the five years of his monopoly, his captains had sailed eastward along the whole length of the Gulf of Guinea, had reached the islands in the Bight of Biafra and had turned southwards once more to cross the Equator. This remarkable series of voyages was briefly summarized by Barros, but we know hardly any of the details of them. We do not know, for instance, whether the Portuguese thought they had reached the southern extremity of the African continent and whether they supposed that the eastward trend of the coast would continue until they sailed into the Indian Ocean. Nor do we know what their feelings were, when, in longitude 9°E or thereabouts, the coast turned once more relentlessly to the southward.

The first expedition dispatched by Gomes seems to have been under the command of that Soeiro da Costa who had sailed with Pêro de Sintra in 1462. He passed Cape Palmas, where the coast makes its definitive turn to the eastward and reached a river temporarily called by his name, but now known as the Assini, near the border between the modern states of the Ivory Coast and Ghana. On this stretch Duarte Pacheco mentions particularly the Rio dos Cestos, the only place where baskets were made. At first an *alqueire* of *malagueta* could be bought here for a single brass ring and a slave for two basins, but a few years later the price had risen to five or six brass rings for the pepper and four or five basins for a slave.

In 1471 João de Santarém and Pêro de Escobar, piloted by Álvaro Esteves, the 'most skilled in his profession in the whole of Spain', reached the gold-bearing rivers in the neighbourhood of Cape Three Points. The first purchases of gold in this area, which was afterwards known as the Gold Coast, were made at a village called Shama. Fernão Gomes himself made huge profits from the trade in gold and so important was it considered that the fortress of El Mina was afterwards built a short distance away to the east and the 'factory' of Axim on the other side of Three Points, not far away to the west.

In 1472 Fernão do Pó discovered the island which now bears his name, though he called it Ilha Formosa, 'the beautiful island'. There is no mention at all in any of the chronicles of the Bay of Benin or any other part of the coast of modern Nigeria. This is low-lying country: a line of sand-bars is backed by lagoons into which many large rivers, including the Delta streams of the Niger, empty themselves. The whole region is densely forested, very marshy and almost devoid of landmarks. There are one or two good harbours, such as 'Lagos of Guinea', but it was to be many years before the Portuguese made any use of them. One can only suppose that the first captains who passed this way, seeing few signs of life and none of suitable landing-places, made no attempt to explore the lagoons and hastened to put this wet, unattractive forest behind them.

The honour of being the first to cross the Equator fell to one Sequeira who, in 1473 or 1474, reached Cabo de Santa Caterina in a latitude of almost 2°S. This cape is almost a hundred miles south of Cape Lopes where the river Ogowe flows into the sea. On the banks of this river, four and a half centuries later, Dr. Schweitzer was to build his hospital at Lambarene. On the way home, Sequeira is thought to have discovered the islands of S. Tomé, S. Antão (now called I. do Principe) and I. do Anno Bom, though this latter island was not officially 'discovered' until 1501.

From these ventures Gomes gained not only great wealth, but great prestige also. After the Arzila campaign he was knighted and, in the last year of his contract, the King ennobled him. He was granted a device of three heads of negroes on a field of silver, each negro with golden rings in his ears and nose and a collar of gold around his neck. But in spite of his success his contract was not renewed in 1474 and the conduct of the affairs of Guinea was handed over to Prince João. It was felt that a private citizen, however rich and powerful, could not defend this huge territory against foreign pirates, especially in view of the King's quarrel with Castile.

It is now time to consider what was happening in Castile. The reign of Henry IV (1454-74) is complicated and un-inspiring, but its plots and counter-plots must be briefly summarized for their effects on the story of overseas exploration. Although at times they bordered on the comic, they brought the Portuguese expeditions to a temporary halt, because the war with their neighbours in which they became involved absorbed all their energies for several years. But in the end these events ushered in the era of Ferdinand and Isabella, *Los Reyes Católicos*, and so contributed to the impact which this celebrated pair were to have on the course of world history.

Henry IV was the son of Juan II. He had a half-brother, Alfonso, and a half-sister, Isabella, both much younger than himself. His first wife was Blanche of Navarre, but this marriage had been annulled on the grounds that he was incapable of fathering children. He himself claimed that his wife was barren. In 1455 he married D. Joana, the sister of King Afonso of Portugal. This glamorous and wayward princess and the covey of chattering girls she brought with her from Portugal greatly scandalized the clerics and nobility of Castile, who, since popular rumour attributed to their King almost every vice in the calendar, had plenty to gossip about already. It was generally agreed that Henry IV was impotent and the surprise of all may be imagined, when, after seven years of marriage, Queen Joana gave birth to a daughter. The child was christened Juana after her mother, but she soon became widely known as *La Beltreneja*, as her father was thought to be D. Beltran de la Cueva, an obscure nobleman who spent most of his time at Court. The King, however, made haste to proclaim her Princess of the Asturias, the title usually held by the heir to the throne. To the disgust of his critics, he also appointed D. Beltran Count of Ledesma, Master of the Order of Santiago and, later on, Duke of Albuquerque.

The King of Castile badly needed an ally. In addition to the growing unrest within his own kingdom, he was on bad terms with the King of Aragon, the father of his first wife. His thoughts naturally turned to Portugal and as early as 1464 he arranged a meeting with D. Afonso at Gibraltar. He suggested that the King of Portugal should marry his half-sister Isabella and that the heir to the Portuguese throne, D. João, should marry the infant Princess Juana. D. Afonso had never intended to marry again, for he had been devoted to his first wife, Isabel, but the prospect of presiding over the union of Castile and Portugal was too dazzling to be ignored.

These negotiations came to nothing, partly, no doubt, because D. Afonso's ill-success in Africa at this time made him seem less desirable as an ally, but more especially because of the antagonism of the Castilian nobility. The King's opponents were by no means at one, but most of them now acknowledged D. Alfonso as heir to the throne and, when he died in 1468, transferred their allegiance to his sister Isabella. They forced King Henry to sign a document in which he agreed to divorce Queen Joana, declare Isabella his heir and so, by inference, admit that D. Juana was illegitimate. But in the midst of all this, Prince Fernando of Aragon suddenly arrived at Valladolid, disguised as a muleteer, and D. Isabella married him. This *coup-de-main* was engineered by the Archbishop of Toledo, but it was not at all to the liking of some of his fellow-conspirators who deserted the newly-wedded bride and joined the Portuguese faction.

In 1474 Henry IV died. In his will he made D. Juana his heir, thereby officially recognizing her legitimacy once more, and begged D. Afonso of Portugal to marry her and govern Castile on her behalf[5].

Throughout this period, it was the secret wish of the rulers of both Castile and Portugal to bring about the union of the two countries. Consequently, for political as well as sentimental reasons, D. Afonso could not resist this appeal to assist his thirteen-year-old niece. It seemed a unique

La Virgén de los Reyes Católicos

Vasco da Gama

opportunity. Although D. Isabella had been crowned at Seville, her position was still very insecure. She was only twenty and many leading Castilians, led by the Marquis de Villena, favoured her rival. Although the views of his councillors were by no means unanimous, D. Afonso decided to invade Castile in support of the claims of his niece. Leaving his son in charge of his kingdom, he marched slowly northwards and occupied Zamora and Toro, two cities on the upper Douro in the heart of Old Castile. A few miles to the east D. Ferdinand of Aragon, with a large but ill-equipped army which he had hastily collected, barred the way to Valladolid.

The campaign then ground to a standstill. The troops which the Marquis de Villena had promised Afonso did not arrive. The ordinary people of Castile did not want a Portuguese king and the nobility were busy guarding their own estates. Many of the Portuguese were equally luke-warm about an affair which they regarded as none of their business. Prince Ferdinand, for his part, was not at all eager to risk a pitched battle with untrained troops, but his wife meanwhile was full of energy and it was not long before, by a mixture of threats and bribes, she succeeded in winning over many of those who had at first opposed her. After several small skirmishes, D. Afonso succeeded in losing Zamora, thus allowing his direct line of retreat to Portugal to be cut. Food and money began to run short; during the winter it was uncomfortably cold and many of his men went home.

In this depressing situation, the King sent for his son, the one person he could really trust. The Prince arrived in February 1476 and shortly afterwards his father decided to make a demonstration in force in the direction of Zamora, since it lay between his own headquarters at Toro and the Portuguese frontier. After camping for some days on the river bank opposite Zamora, D. Afonso changed his mind and began to withdraw just as Prince Fernando decided to attack him. These manoeuvres led to the curious battle of Toro. As the old Roman bridge over the Douro at Zamora is very narrow, it took Ferdinand most of the day to get his troops across to the south bank and it was late in the afternoon before he caught up with the Portuguese. His left wing beside the river drove back D. Afonso in disorder, but, on the Portuguese left, Prince João was equally successful. As by this time it was pitch-dark, misty and pouring with rain, no one knew what had actually happened. But next morning D. João, who had kept a close grip on his men, was found to be encamped in good order on the battlefield; Prince Ferdinand's army, both victors and vanquished, had dribbled back into Zamora; D. Afonso had disappeared. It was only in the afternoon that it transpired that he had taken refuge in a nearby castle.

Both sides claimed a victory, but, although D. João's performance could not be faulted, his father's prestige had suffered badly and most of the Castilian *hidalgos* hastened to make their peace with Queen Isabella. Nevertheless, D. Afonso would not give up. He had been exchanging letters with Louis XI of France who had his eye on part of the kingdom of Aragon. He convinced himself that it only needed a personal explanation to bring Louis into the war on his side. He forthwith decided to abandon his army and his kingdom and set out for France. At first Louis welcomed his unexpected visitor enthusiastically: he thought he might be useful in his quarrel with Charles the Bold, Duke of Burgundy, since Charles was the son of Philip the Good and Isabel of Portugal and therefore a close relation of D. Afonso. But after the defeat and death of the Duke in January 1477, Louis lost interest and the

nfortunate D. Afonso wandered about France for several
nonths while his host put him off with various excuses.
aced with the failure of both his war in Castile and his
iplomacy in France, he could not bear to return home.
t last, in September 1477, when he had already been
way for over a year, he made up his mind to abdicate and
ke to the life of a wandering religious. Leaving letters for
is son, the nobility of Portugal and his companions, he
isappeared one night from Harfleur with five retainers
n route for Jerusalem.

His retinue were horrified. Louis, greatly put out at
nislaying his royal guest, ordered him to be found at
nce. After some days he was run to earth asleep in a way-
ide tavern and Louis at once packed him off home to
ortugal. Meanwhile, D. João had managed to hold his
wn. Although in Castile D. Juana's supporters had been
orced to surrender one by one, attempts by the Isabelines
o invade the border regions of Alentejo had been success-
ully foiled. But the kingdom's finances were in a desperate
tate and D. João was planning to present to the Cortes
uggestions for a special levy when he received his father's
etter of abdication. After much heart-searching, the Prince
greed to accept the Crown, but the celebrations were
carcely over when the ship with D. Afonso on board put
nto the Tagus. D. João hastened to restore to his father
he position he had held for four days.

Back home once more, D. Afonso cheered up and it
vas not long before messengers were galloping to and fro
cross the frontier with grandiose plans for renewing the
var. But D. João, although he always treated his father
vith the greatest respect, had no intention of letting slip the
eins of authority which he had held for so long nor of
olunging the country further into debt. Nevertheless, the
var dragged on. Almost everyone was heartily sick of it,

but no one seemed to be able to think of a way of bringin
it to an end. Finally, through the intervention of I
Beatriz, who was D. João's mother-in-law, but also th
aunt of Isabella of Castile, the two sides were brough
together. The Treaty of Alcaçovas was signed on 4th Sep
tember 1479 and ratified at Toledo in the following March

The conditions of peace, though signed in the name c
D. Afonso, were actually negotiated by his son. The Kin
of Portugal and the Queen of Castile agreed to give u
their claims to each other's territories, since it was clea
that the union of the two countries, which they both s
much desired, could not be achieved by war. But neithe
side was prepared to abandon the hope that it might b
brought about by peaceful means. As a guarantee of goo
faith, D. João's son Afonso, who was four years old i
1479, and D. Isabella, eldest child of *Los Reyes Católico*
who was five years older, were to be entrusted to the ca
of D. Beatriz in her castle at Moura on the Portugues
frontier. As soon as they were old enough, these tw
children were to be married, so that their heir would hav
an undisputed claim to the thrones of both Castile an
Portugal and, it was hoped, Aragon as well. These arrange
ments came into effect in January 1481 and were know
as *As Terçarias de Moura*.

D. Juana's supporters in Castile were to be pardone
and their titles and estates restored to them. But the claim
of D. Juana herself were ungallantly set aside. She was t
become a nun, unless she agreed to her betrothal to th
one-year-old son of Ferdinand and Isabella. At eightee
this was an indignity she could not accept and she chos
to enter the Convent of Santa Clara at Coimbra. No longe
Queen of Castile, Leon and Portugal, nor even Princes
she was known for the forty remaining years of her life a
A Excelente Senhora.

During the war Queen Isabella had ignored the Papal ban
on voyages beyond Cape Bojador and had encouraged her
sailors both to trade with Guinea and to attack Portuguese
ships on their way home from African waters. D. João was
determined to regain the monopoly which he considered his
by right and the relevant clauses of the Treaty of Alcaçovas
were designed to settle outstanding disputes once and for
all. 'The Lordship of Guinea', it read, 'belongs to the King
of Portugal, and all its regions, lands and markets, together
with its gold mines, both those discovered or to be discovered, spoken of or to be spoken of, and including the
islands of Madeira, Porto Santo and Deserta, the Açores
and Las Flores, the Cape Verde Islands, and all the islands
which have been discovered, mentioned or conquered
from the Canaries southward to Guinea – saving only the
Canary Islands, which occupied or as yet unoccupied,
belong to the Crown of Castile . . . And if any of the inhabitants of Castile, or any foreigners, whoever they may
be, shall go to trade, hinder, damage, rob or conquer the
said Guinea, its regions, commerce, mines, land or islands,
discovered or to be discovered, without the express licence
and consent of the King or Prince of Portugal or their
successors, they shall be punished in such manner, place or
form as shall be laid down in the treaty and in accordance
with the laws of the sea against those who land on the coast,
beaches, harbours or ports to rob, damage or do evil, or
those who commit these misdeeds on the open sea[6].'

The treaty further laid down that the conquest of the
Kingdom of Fez was the exclusive right of the King of
Portugal and his successors, but that the Canaries and the
Kingdom of Granada belonged exclusively to the Queen
of Castile and her successors.

Although without question Portugal had lost the war
the terms of the peace treaty represented a personal triumph

for the young D. João. He had already proved himself
brave and resourceful soldier and by his special appeal h
had saved his country from bankruptcy. Now he showe
himself an able and resolute diplomatist. His future sul
jects, except for the Duke of Bragança and his friend
admired him greatly. They called him *O Principe Perfeit*
'The Perfect Prince'.

In August 1481, King Afonso V died. He was onl
forty-nine, but since his return from France he had age
rapidly and lived in semi-retirement at a Franciscan mona
tery near Torres Vedras. He had been deeply humiliate
yet once more by the treatment accorded to D. Juana an
had seen his dearest ambitions finally in ruins. Yet to th
end he seems to have loved and trusted his son and to hav
been intensely proud of him. Poor man, it was the onl
thing he had left to be proud of!

8

The Perfect Prince

With the death of Afonso V, the nobility of Portugal had lost a kindly and generous patron. They looked forward to the future with some misgiving. They were dominated by the Braganças and by the children of D. Beatriz, widow of D. Fernão, younger brother of the late King. These two families were closely related to each other, to the King and to the royal house of Castile. The leader of the Bragança clan was now Fernão, the third Duke, an arrogant grandee of about fifty, who had recently succeeded to the title. Immensely wealthy in his own right, he could also call on the support of his three brothers, the Marquis of Montenor, the Count of Faro and D. Álvaro who, though he had no title, had been appointed Chancellor by Afonso V. But, as will be seen from the genealogical table on p. 11, D. Beatriz was at the centre of this web of relationships. She was the King's aunt by marriage: she was also his mother-in-law. She was also the mother-in-law of the Duke of Bragança. She was the aunt of Isabella the Catholic. She was the granddaughter of D. João I and on her mother's side she was also his great-grand-daughter, through the first Duke of Bragança. She had had nine children: five had died young, but her two surviving sons, the Duke of Viseu and the twelve-year-old Manuel, the future Duke of Beja, were next in line to the throne after the King's own son, Prince Afonso.

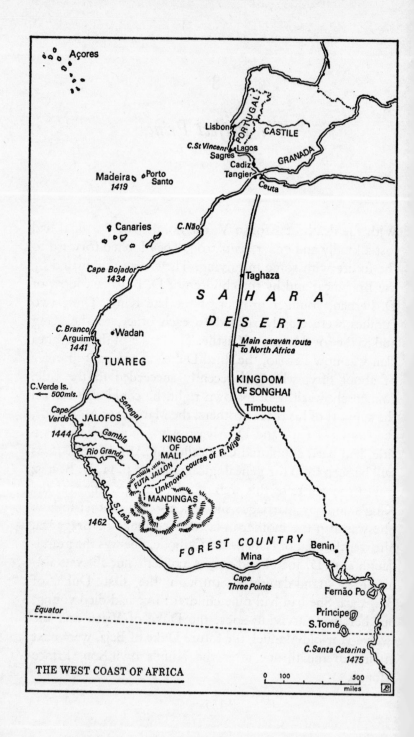

THE WEST COAST OF AFRICA

Açores

Lisbon
PORTUGAL
CASTILE
C.St Vincent
Lagos
Sagres
Cadiz
GRANADA
Tangier
Ceuta

Madeira
1419
Porto
Santo

Canaries
C.Não

Cape Bojador
1434

Taghaza

S A H A R A
D E S E R T

C.Branco
Arguim
1441
Wadan

Main caravan route
to North Africa

TUAREG

KINGDOM
OF SONGHAI

C.Verde Is.
← 500 mls.

Senegal

Cape
Verde
JALOFOS
1444

Timbuctu

Gambía

KINGDOM
OF
MALI

Rio Grande

Unknown course of R. Niger

FUTA JALLON

MANDINGAS

S. Leôa

1462

FOREST COUNTRY
Benin
Mina

Cape
Three Points

Fernão Po

Equator

Principe
S.Tomé

C.Santa Catarina
1475

THE WEST COAST OF AFRICA

0   100   500
miles

The fears of the nobility were soon realized. In November 1481, the third month of his reign, the King held a meeting of the Cortes. He not only exacted from the *fidalgos* a much more rigorous oath of allegiance than had been customary in the past, but demanded proofs of the grants and privileges which each of them claimed and of the titles by which each of them held lands, fortresses or castles. Moreover, as if this were not enough, he openly encouraged the representatives of the people when they began to voice their grievances. Among other complaints, the delegates declared that many landowners were in the habit of levying extra taxes without authority; that they commonly interfered with the course of justice and that they compelled poor people to work for them without payment. They asked the King to extend the system of royal magistrates (*corregidores*) throughout the kingdom and, in the interests of economy, to reduce the crowd of pensioners and hangers-on who thronged the Court. Instead of ignoring such criticism, as his father had done, the King promised them redress.

Bragança was greatly enraged by these happenings, especially by the appointment of *corregidores* who would tread heavily on his ducal prerogatives. He found it difficult to believe that this, or any other of the King's decisions, could possibly apply to him. But when he saw that it apparently was so, he sent off at once to his castle at Vila Vicosa for the documents which would prove what rights and privileges had been granted to his family over the last seventy years. By an extraordinary piece of carelessness, he failed to ensure that all who had access to his archives were trustworthy, and some of his private correspondence fell into the hands of the King. This revealed that for some time the Duke had been in touch with Isabella of Castile and was encouraging her to lay claim to the throne of Portugal. Furthermore, it showed the King that the Duke's brothers, D. Beatriz and her son, the Duke of Viseu, were all aware of the plot.

Now that he knew where to look, D. João was able to arrange for copies of all the Duke's secret correspondence to be brought to him. But although these provided certain proof of the Duke's disloyalty, the King's hands were tied by the *terçarias* and by the painful knowledge that D. Beatriz, the guardian of his much loved son and heir, was among those who were suspect. He set himself the task of persuading Isabella that she now had nothing to fear from Portugal and that the arrangements for the *terçarias* could be dispensed with. For D. João there followed long and anxious negotiations. Although Isabella missed her daughter as much as D. João missed his son, she was by no means convinced that all danger from the Infanta Juana had passed. The Duke of Bragança, from his stronghold at Vila Vicosa, close to the frontier, advised delay. But eventually agreement was reached and, amid great rejoicings, Prince Afonso rejoined his parents in May 1483.

Earlier in the year the King had hinted to Bragança that he was aware of his dealings with Castile, but the Duke, secure in the knowledge that the evidence was safely locked away in his private chest, had taken no notice. Now D. João struck at once. A week after the Prince arrived at Évora, the Duke was placed under arrest. As soon as the King had received the surrender of the Bragança castles, and was sure that Ferdinand and Isabella would make no move, he declared that the Duke must be formally tried for treason. With the evidence of the letters, there could be only one verdict and the Duke was executed on 20th June 1483.

At the trial and when the news of the execution was

brought to him, the King is said to have wept bitterly.

Although the Duke was dead, the conspiracy was not. It was kept alive by a group of disgruntled nobles who had flourished under Afonso V and who found little to their liking a régime where royal favours were distributed strictly on merit. Indeed the King was in greater danger than before. The Braganças were masters of intrigue: by such means the first Duke had brought about the downfall of D. Pedro in 1448; the third Duke had no doubt also hoped to manoeuvre D. João into making some fatal mistake. But the new conspirators favoured direct action. They intended to kill the King, eliminate Prince Afonso and put D. Diogo, Duke of Viseu, on the throne. This young man had much in common with his uncle, Afonso V: he was greatly taken with his own importance; he submitted ungraciously to discipline and he was easily led by those who flattered him.

D. Diogo was of the blood royal. He could not be tried by the courts as the Duke of Bragança had been tried. To save his life and his kingdom, the King must do what had to be done himself. He summoned his cousin to his private apartments at Setúbal and there, in the presence of three loyal councillors, stabbed him to death.

This tragedy finally destroyed the opposition to the throne. Of the other leading conspirators, some were arrested and executed, others fled to Castile. But the King was still left with the task of justifying himself to D. Beatriz and to the Queen, the mother and sister of the dead man. It was, perhaps, because of this that he was generous to D. Manuel, now the only surviving son of D. Beatriz. He granted him all his brother's property and estates with the title of Duke of Beja, he gave him the Lordship of the islands of the Ocean which D. Henrique had bequeathed to his father, D. Fernão; lastly, he promised that if his own son, Prince Afonso, should die, he would be the heir to the throne.

Meanwhile D. João had already turned his attention to Africa. Although the affairs of Guinea had already been in his hands for several years, no new discoveries of any importance had been made since the contract of Fernão Gomes had expired in 1474. Even while he was forced to keep one eye on the Duke of Bragança, he was already making preparations for a fresh expedition which was to continue the search for the southern extremity of Africa. But one thing was more important than new discoveries, and that was the protection of what he already had. The products of Guinea and especially the gold from 'Elmina' were something which the merchants of other countries could not resist. To obtain them, they were ready to brave the wrath of the Pope and ignore the Treaty of Alcaçovas.

There were, no doubt, many voyages of which we have no record, but we do know that in 1479 a Frenchman called Eustace de la Fosse sailed for Elmina from a Spanish port. He was unlucky enough to be intercepted by Diogo Cão; his goods were confiscated, his ship was impounded and he and his crew brought home prisoners to Lisbon. In 1475, says Duarte Pacheco, 'there was fitted out in Flanders a Flemish ship with a Castilian pilot and divers merchandise. They were resolved to go to Guinea to trade and to defy the prohibitions of the Holy Father who had granted these lands to the King of Portugal, so that none might go there without the permission of the said King. But because these Flemings had set at nought the edicts of the Pastor of the Holy Mother Church, God willed them a cruel fate. For, on the return voyage from Elmina, when they had loaded goods to the value of six *dobras*, they came abreast of the Beach of Slaves. And there, because the wind had dropped, they cast anchor in deep water. And during the night the wind rose and the anchor dragged. And because the bottom was foul, a rock cut the cable and they were driven onto the shore and wrecked. And the negroes ate all the thirty-five Flemings who were in the ship. This we know from Pedro Gonçalves, who was told the story by the natives when he visited the coast in the following year. He brought back all the gold which the Flemings had collected together with some of their clothing[1].'

D. João did not feel that he could rely on his merchant captains to keep the coast free of interlopers nor indeed could he always trust in the intervention of providence. He saw that a permanent base was needed and decided to build and maintain a fort to safeguard the treasures of Elmina. He chose for this enterprise D. Diogo de Azambuja and, within a few months of his accession, dispatched him to the Gold Coast with what amounted to a prefabricated fort. His instructions were to choose a suitable site and to build on it a 'factory' and a fortress for the encouragement and protection of trade. If possible, he was to secure the agreement of the local people; if necessary, he must do without it. He must be prepared to be a diplomat or a soldier.

The King was generally well served by the men he chose for important missions, for he was a good judge of character. D. Diogo was one of his most trustworthy servants; later he was to be one of the three witnesses to the death of the Duke of Viseu described on a previous page. In this case, he carried out his instructions to the letter. The place he selected for the fortress of São Jorge da Mina, the first European settlement in tropical Africa, was a sheltered bay about sixty miles west of the modern town of Accra. It was protected by a lofty cape on which the fortress could be built; a large village close to the edge of the forest told them that there was plenty of fresh water near by and in the bay a Portuguese caravel commanded by João Bernardes lay at anchor.

This Bernardes was a great help. He was on good terms with the natives, he spoke their language and he could assure his countrymen that gold from the mines could be obtained there in plenty. On the next day, therefore, D. Diogo and his officers dressed themselves in their best and went on shore. They heard Mass and dined under a huge tree by the water's edge. They made themselves ready to meet Chief Caramansa. D. Diogo, gleaming with jewels, sat in a chair of honour which had been brought from the ship for the purpose. His men stood in two long ranks in front of him. Previously, the natives had seen only tough merchant captains and their uncouth crews in their working clothes. This colourful charade of full fifteenth-century court dress filled them with astonishment.

But Caramansa was not to be outdone. He marched in procession from his village, moving with the slow, dignified gait of African royalty. His musicians led the way with horns and rattles and drums. On either side his bodyguard brandished their bows and spears. He was bedecked with gold, his wrists and ankles were encircled with gold bracelets, golden beads hung from his hair and little bells jangled as he walked.

D. Diogo greeted the Chief with great solemnity and, with Bernardes as his interpreter, he made a speech. 'The King of Portugal, my master', he said, 'has heard such good reports of the great Chief Caramansa that he has sent me to offer him a treaty of alliance and friendship. Other rulers in this region of Africa have sought this privilege, but only to him has the Great Lord of Portugal granted it. He alone has merited such friendship and confidence and the wealth and happiness it will surely bring. But, so that these things may come to pass, it will be necessary to build a great house in which the merchandise which is brought here can be lodged. In this way, the trade which has already begun between white and black will increase and prosper. And if he consents, I, Diogo, will set to work on the building immediately[2].'

Caramansa was doubtful. He was not sure about a 'great house'. Had not the system of barter so far proved satisfactory and profitable? Was it wise to change it? Friends could see too much of each other. And in any case, who was this great Lord with his fine clothes and fair speech? Was he a brother or a nephew of the King of Portugal?

Amid much hand-clapping and wails of astonishment, D. Diogo informed him blandly that in his country the King had more than two hundred thousand vassals, richer, nobler and more elegant than himself. Caramansa agreed that the 'great house' might be built. 'After all,' he added philosophically, 'if such close neighbours prove inconvenient, the forest is wide and a new village can easily be built elsewhere.'

After this ceremony, D. Diogo lost no time in landing the materials which had been brought from Portugal and setting his men to work. But they had hardly reached the chosen site before they were surrounded by a crowd of angry, excited Africans, brandishing their spears and all talking at once. It was with the greatest difficulty that the Portuguese could find out what the trouble was, but at last they learnt that the villagers held in veneration the rocks on the headland and that the workmen were trespassing on sacred ground. It may well have been that this, the nearest high ground, was a burial place and that the natives feared the anger of their ancestors if they were disturbed.

A calamity was only averted by the prompt dispatch of a generous present to Caramansa. After this, things went more smoothly. Many of the tribesmen came to help, prepared to risk the wrath of their deities in return for the exciting objects with which the Portuguese paid them. More presents satisfied those who had to move their huts off the headland. A spring was found within the circuit of the walls of the new fort. Within three weeks the tower was complete and part of the building was habitable. A church was rising near by. A few Portuguese had died of disease, but the climate had proved less deadly than had been expected.

D. Diogo kept sixty men with him to garrison the fort and sent the rest back to Portugal. He himself remained at S. Jorge for more than two years. His mission had been entirely successful. Good relations had been established with the Chief and his people and it was not long before gold began to flow down the forest tracks to the new factory.

While D. Diogo de Azambuja was thus engaged, the King was deep in preparations for a new expedition which would explore the coasts of Africa beyond the furthest point yet reached. It was more than ten years since the ships of Fernão Gomes had crossed the Equator and the Portuguese were still no nearer knowing whether the Indies could be reached by sea than they had been in the time of Henry the Navigator. It had been a great disappointment to them when, beyond the eastern limits of Guinea, the coast had turned inexorably southward again and they had to admit that the way to the Arabian Sea did not yet lie open. Nevertheless, D. João seems to have been able to convince himself that it was only a matter of time before his ships would at last turn the southernmost cape of Africa.

He chose for this new enterprise Diogo Cão, an experienced captain who has already been mentioned in connection with the capture of Eustace de la Fosse. Cão has received from posterity less than his due. In the space of five years he added more than sixteen hundred miles of coastline to the map of Africa; he discovered and explored the lower reaches of the Congo and he visited an African monarch more powerful than any his countrymen had so far encountered. Yet there is no contemporary record of his two voyages and even the dates of them and the sequence of events are obscure. Writing only twenty years later, Duarte Pacheco mentions few details and only one voyage.

It may be that D. João himself was responsible for this uncertainty. In the hope of concealing his new discoveries from the outside world, and especially from his neighbours in Castile, he is generally supposed to have ordered all the records to be deposited in the archives where they were eventually destroyed in the Lisbon earthquake of 1755. If this indeed was his intention, he was only partially successful, since it was always possible for his rivals to lure Portuguese pilots away from their allegiance or to arrange, at a price, for Portuguese maps to be smuggled out of the country. The Soligo map fell into the hands of the Duke of Este in this way.

It seems most likely that Cão set out in the spring of 1482, shortly after the news was received of the successful completion of the fort at S. Jorge da Mina. At any rate he called there to take on food and water. Beyond Cape Santa Caterina, a few miles south of the Equator, he began to break new ground and by August he had reached the mouth of the mighty Congo. He called it the Rio Poderoso, but it was more usually known as the Zaire, which was the native name for it, or the Rio Padrão, the River of the Pillar. It had been the custom for Portuguese captains to set up wooden pillars or crosses to mark prominent points on their voyages, but these soon rotted away or were cut down. So Diogo Cão was provided with stone pillars decorated with the arms of Portugal and a short inscription in praise of the King and of the captain himself. Cão erected the first of these pillars at the mouth of the Congo[3].

The people of the populous villages near the estuary seemed friendly, but they spoke a language which no one on board could understand. It was with some difficulty, therefore, that the Portuguese learnt that they were the subjects of the Manicongo, who ruled his vast kingdom from his capital at Ambasse, fifty leagues away inland. In accordance with his instructions, Cão dispatched an embassy with presents for the King and a friendly message from D. João. His ambassadors disappeared into the forest and their leader settled down to await their return. As the months passed, he grew impatient to continue his voyage. In the end he seized hostages from the villagers who daily visited his ship and, leaving a message that he intended to return, set out once more for the south. He did not return for nearly three years and the feelings of his men when at last they returned to the coast from the Manicongo's capital may be imagined.

Meanwhile, at 13°26'S, on a promontory now called Cape Santa Maria, Diogo Cão had erected the pillar of S. Agostinho. This pillar, after weathering four hundred

ears on the Atlantic coast of Africa, was brought back to
Lisbon in 1892. It is the only evidence for this part of the
voyage, but it is to be presumed that then, or shortly
afterwards, Cão turned for home. He was greeted with
the greatest enthusiasm by D. João; he was knighted and
awarded a generous pension. The King was clearly convinced that the southernmost cape of Africa lay close at
hand. It is difficult to see why he should have been so
confident. The coast at Cape Santa Maria runs south-
south-west and continues to do so for many miles. Perhaps the pillar does not represent the furthest point reached
on this voyage and Cão reported an eastward trend to
the coast much further to the south. Perhaps D. João and
his advisers put their faith in those classical geographers
who placed the Promontorium Prassum, the ultimate cape
of Africa, in approximately the latitude which had now
been reached. Whatever their reasons, they were sufficiently
convincing for the Portuguese envoy to the Papacy to hint
in public that the sea route to the Arabian Sea had now
been found[4] and for Soligo's map to show the coastline
bearing sharply to the eastward beyond the pillar of S.
Agostinho[5].

In view of the importance of putting these theories to the
test, it is surprising that Diogo Cão did not, apparently, set
out on his second voyage until the autumn of 1485. But the
King had first of all to deal with the conspiracy of the Duke
of Viseu and then with the importunities of Christopher
Columbus who had just made his first appearance at the
Portuguese Court. The ideas of Columbus and their effect
on Portuguese policies will be discussed in a later chapter,
but D. João must have considered very carefully whether
the suggested route to the Indies across the western ocean
might not be very much shorter than that by southern
Africa. But once the decision had been taken, Cão was

told to lose no time. He had with him the celebrated pilot Pêro de Escobar, and the four Congolese hostages from the previous voyage, now richly clothed at the King's expense and chattering happily in Portuguese. Cão put them ashore at the mouth of the Congo and took on board his messengers to the Manicongo who seemed to have survived unharmed their three-year exile. But now a bitter disappointment awaited him. Whatever he may have thought himself or whatever he may have told the King, it was soon clear that the legendary southern cape had not been reached. At 15°42'S he went ashore at Cape Negro to set up a pillar. But soon he began to leave behind the populous forests of the Congo region and to enter a zone which reminded him of the desert lands of north-west Africa. The land grew drier, more desolate and uninviting. Inland a range of barren mountains ran parallel with the sea. Cão called them the Serra Parda, the Grey Mountains. Offshore there were rocks and hidden shoals. The wind blew steadily against them from the south-east and the unfavourable currents grew stronger. Food was running short and they could not easily find places to fill their water-casks. They struggled on almost to the Tropic of Capricorn and in 21°50'S they raised their last pillar at a point which is known to this day as Cape Cross.

With a heavy heart Diogo Cão turned back. He still had to visit the Manicongo and offer him a treaty of friendship and alliance with the King of Portugal. From the mouth of the Congo, he sailed upstream to the Yelala falls and there he and members of his crew carved their names on a nearby rock where they can still be seen. It is to be presumed that he had learnt that from the falls he could shorten the overland journey to Ambasse; he may even have hoped to reach the capital by water.

The Manicongo was delighted to see him. He had been

greatly interested, Rui de Pina tells us, in the tales the four hostages had brought back from Portugal and never tired of asking them about their adventures. He accepted graciously the presents which Cão brought with him and hastened to agree that he was ready, and even eager, to embrace the Christian faith. He would send an ambassador to his brother of Portugal and he chose for this mission Caçuta, one of the hostages who spoke Portuguese well. Let him be baptized and let the King of Portugal send him priests and friars to instruct his people; farmers, oxen and cows so that the agriculture of his country could be improved; teachers so that the children could learn to read and write and even women so that the women of his kingdom could learn to bake bread. 'The kingdom of the Congo', he said, 'shall be like Portugal in Africa.'

In Lisbon, Caçuta was received with all honour. When he came to be baptized, King João and his Queen stood as god-parents. But from the moment he took leave of the Manicongo, Diogo Cão disappears from the records of the chroniclers. It has been suggested that he died on the way home or that D. João threw him into prison for his failure to reach the Promised Land. This does not seem very likely, for the King, though severe, was not unjust. But whatever happened to Cão, D. João himself seems to have come to two conclusions: first, that it was more than ever important that the results of this voyage should be kept secret; and secondly, that, though they were somewhat disappointing, they were sufficiently promising to be followed up as soon as possible. Now that he had sent Columbus about his business, he must open up the route to the Indies by way of southern Africa without delay. He could not afford to fail.

He chose Bartolemeu Dias to lead the new venture[6]. We

do not know exactly when he set out, but it must have been some months after the return of Diogo Cão from his second voyage, a date which is itself uncertain. The most likely guess seems to be the early summer of 1487.

While the little fleet of two caravels and a store-ship were being got ready, the most exhaustive discussions must have been going on. The King, like his great-uncle, had technical advisers, mathematicians, astronomers, cartographers and shipwrights, who considered how every difficulty that Cão had reported might be overcome. Because caravels were so small, he had run short of food and water, so Dias was given a store-ship which could, if necessary, be abandoned. There was no way yet of determining longitude, but Dias was provided with tables of the declination of the sun prepared by José Visinho, so that when, in the southern hemisphere, the Pole Star disappeared over the horizon, he could more easily calculate his latitude. Cão had reported contrary winds and currents beyond the River of the Pillar, which grew stronger as he sailed southwards. Since the days of Henry the Navigator, sailors returning from Guinea had avoided the northerly winds and currents off the north-west coast of Africa by sailing out into the Atlantic to the neighbourhood of the Açores and there picking up the westerlies which carried them home to Portugal. Was it possible that the southerly winds and currents which were to be met with in the same latitudes south of the Equator could be avoided in the same way, by sailing south-west into the Atlantic and picking up a westerly wind which would carry them back to the coast of Africa or even beyond it into the Arabian Sea?[7]

We know nothing of such discussions even from Duarte Pacheco who, as one of the most celebrated geographers of his time, may well have been present at them. We only know what Bartolemeu Dias did. With Pêro de Alenquer as his pilot and João Infante and his own brother in command of the other vessels, he called, as usual, at S. Jorge da Mina. At various points on the coast he put ashore African men and women who had been instructed to explore the country and bring back news of it for the King. He sailed on past the mouth of the Congo and past the pillar which Diogo Cão had erected at Cape Cross, mapping and naming every inlet and headland on the coast. About Christmas they dropped anchor in a sheltered bay in 29°S. The wind now blew briskly from the south-south-west; even the caravels could make little headway and it was clear that the store-ship must remain where she was with nine chosen men to look after her. For Dias and his officers this was the moment of decision. Should they risk their lives in the open Atlantic, in the hope of finding the westerlies which might, or might not, exist to blow them back to Africa? After five more days of beating against the southerly winds, they made up their minds. For many days the two cockle-shells sailed south-west into the unknown; then south-wards through a belt of variable winds, until, at 40°S, or thereabouts, there were the westerlies to carry them back in the direction they wanted to go. Many more days passed and then, after anxious calculations, for they could only estimate longitude by dead reckoning, they decided that they were further east than the line on which the coast of Africa should lie. Full of curiosity, they turned north-wards and, as the mountains came over the horizon towards them, they saw that the coastline ran from west to east with a touch of north.

They made their landfall in what is now called Mossel Bay. In the pleasant warmth of the southern summer, they dropped anchor in a sheltered cove which they called Angra dos Vaqueiros. For in the open glades beyond the sandy shore, herds of small, humped cattle grazed, watched by small grey men with curly hair. But they could make no contact with these Hottentot herdsmen who fled as they approached into the scrub which covered the hillsides and only returned to greet the watering party with showers of arrows.

Dias and his men sailed on eastwards. They still could not be entirely certain that the ultimate cape had been reached, for beyond Mossel Bay the coast runs a few points south of east and two great promontories jut out into the ocean. But at last they reached the bay where Port Elizabeth now stands. The coast turned sharply north-eastward and the waters of a tropical current bathed their ship. There could be no further doubt.

But now the crews would go no further and even the officers counselled caution. Dias persuaded them to give him three more days and at last from the Rio Infante, so called because João Infante led the way into the estuary, he had to turn back.

After an absence of more than a year, Dias sailed into the Tagus towards the end of 1488. On his way home, he had picked up three of the little party who had been left to guard the store-ship; the rest had been killed by the natives and one of the survivors, Barros tells us, had died of joy at the moment of rescue. He could report not only that he had entered the Arabian Sea, but also that on his homeward voyage he had passed the Promontorium Prassum of the ancients. He called it Cabo Tormentoso, because even in the summer months the waves broke over the rocks below it in clouds of spray. But the King said it should be called Cabo de Boa Esperança, Cape of Good Hope, because they could now look forward with high hopes to reaching their goal in the Indies.

Yet Dias received no public honour nor tribute to his success. Before Vasco da Gama set out to bring his efforts to a triumphant conclusion, nine years had passed. By that time D. João was dead and his cousin, Manuel the Fortunate, was King.

9

The Search for Prester John

It will be remembered that Henry the Navigator had been much interested in the legend of Prester John and had hoped that his captains would encounter some Christian king in Africa who would help in his struggle against Islam. Since that time geographical knowledge had much improved: the Portuguese themselves had mapped the whole western coast of Africa and information from Arabic sources had made possible a more realistic version of the shores of the Indian Ocean. The land of Prester John had been firmly identified with Ethiopia and from time to time Coptic monks appeared in Jerusalem or even in Rome to confirm that the ruler of Ethiopia and his subjects were indeed Christians.

But there was still a good deal of confusion in the use of geographical terms. The name 'Indies' was often applied not only to the whole of maritime Asia including China, but also to the countries which bordered on the Indian Ocean, including East Africa. At the same time, 'Ethiopia' was often synonymous with the whole of Africa south of the Sahara. Cartographers showed it stretching far to the south and west to include the sources of the Nile, which, after Ptolemy, they placed well below the Equator in lakes which drew their water from the Mountains of the Moon. It was generally believed that Prester John ruled over a vast empire of subject peoples: seven kings, it was said, constantly attended him at his Court, and sixty dukes;

thirty archbishops sat on the right hand of his throne and twenty bishops on his left.

Presumably D. João himself did not believe all these tales, but he certainly realized that the existence of a friendly kingdom in eastern Africa would be of the greatest help to his plans. Even before Dias reached the Cape, it was already clear that the voyage to the Indies, if it proved to be possible at all, would be exceedingly long and difficult and ports of call would be needed where his captains could find food and fresh water and where they could repair their ships and rigging. D. João hoped that it might be possible to make contact with this mysterious Christian potentate before Portuguese ships actually arrived off his shores. He therefore told his captains to make inquiries wherever they landed and dispatched a stream of messengers into the interior. It was only when these moves came to nothing that he decided on a direct approach to the Empire of Ethiopia by way of Egypt and the Red Sea.

In other respects Portuguese policies had not greatly changed. It was still their intention to encourage trade with the newly-discovered lands and to introduce pagan peoples to the blessings of Christianty. Consequently, in the reigns of D. João and his successors, they learnt a great deal about the interior of Africa, much more than is generally recognized. But, since most of their records lay buried in the archives, it was left to nineteenth-century explorers to unravel the system of lakes and rivers which so puzzled the map-makers of Europe. It so happened that in the fifteenth century much of central Africa was enjoying a period of relative stability. The era of the Bantu warrior tribes was yet to come and their ancestors had built up a number of loosely-knit confederacies of great size. Although tropical diseases must have taken their toll then as later, on the whole communications were slightly better than they afterwards became and travelling a little safer. But in spite of these advantages, D. João could glean little information to help him in his search for Prester John.

The trade through Elmina soon began to show profits, but the new fort did not prove, as might have been expected, a useful base for the exploration of the interior. The local chiefs were determined to keep the carrying trade to themselves. In this period only a single visit to the kingdom of Songhai is recorded. There, King Mohammed bin Maragal, a staunch Muslim, denied all knowledge of a Christian king in his part of Africa. He and his forbears, he said, knew only the kings of neighbouring territories and the Sultan of Cairo. It is tantalizing to have so few details of such an important journey, for at this time the Songhai Empire covered a vast area from its capital at Gao up the Niger to the west and far into the Sahara to the north. It is to be presumed that Mohammed bin Maragal of the chronicles is Mohammed Abubakr, chief minister to Sonni Ali II, who, after his master's death in 1492, seized the throne and took the title of Askia Mohammed.

In the delta kingdom of Benin, reached by João Afonso de Aveiro in 1483, the Christian faith could make no headway against the wishes of its Muslim ruler. But the trading prospects were sufficiently bright to justify the opening of a 'factory' at Gwato, at the western end of the tangled mass of streams which afterwards turned out to be the mouths of the Niger. But many Portuguese died in this unhealthy spot and it was soon abandoned in favour of the off-shore islands of Sao Tomé and Fernando Po. There are still in existence bronzes from Benin, depicting through African eyes these early visitors from Portugal, and a selection of them can be seen in the British Museum.

Meanwhile João Afonso had picked up some exciting

news which caused him to bring home a native of the country to explain matters to his master. It appeared that the kings of Benin, when first they ascended the throne, must send ambassadors with valuable presents to the Prince Ogané to seek his approval to their succesion. This Prince Ogané ruled over a mighty empire far to the east, so far that it took the envoys twenty months to reach it.

'As a sign of his approval', writes Barros[1], 'the Prince Ogané used to send to the Kings of Benin, not a sceptre and a crown, but a helmet of shining brass such as the Spaniards wear, and a staff of the same metal. He sent them also a cross of brass to wear on their heart. And all the time the ambassadors were at the Court of Ogané they never caught sight of the Prince; they saw only silk curtains behind which he placed himself. And when the time came to say good-bye, he showed one foot beneath the curtain to satisfy them that he was there and to this foot they made reverence as to a holy thing. And when he presented the insignia of office, the leader of the embassy received a small cross of the kind sent to the king. And', adds Barros, 'I can write of these things with the more truth because in 1540 there came to this kingdom an embassy from Benin and among them there was an old man of seventy years of age who had one of these crosses and who, on being questioned, told me what I have written above.'

It was disappointing that the realm of Prester John seemed so vague and remote. It was also disappointing that the Muslim rulers of inner Guinea, while they were generally friendly, showed no desire to adopt Christianity themselves, nor to allow missionary work among their pagan subjects. The case of Bemoi, therefore, was all the more welcome. This chief was 'Regent' of a Jaloff kingdom on the Senegal river. In times of prosperity he had encouraged his people to trade with the Portuguese and, when he was driven out by his half-brother, he took refuge with them at the fort at Arguim. The commander of the fort sent him to Portugal where D. João made much of him and he and his five companions were soon delighting their hosts with displays of bare-back riding. It was not long before Bemoi expressed a wish to be baptized and at this event the King and Queen stood as his sponsors. The chance of a Christian ally in Africa was too good to miss. A fleet of twenty caravels was assembled to escort him back to his country and to restore him to his rightful position. But the affair had an unhappy ending. The captain of the fleet, Pêro Vaz da Cunha, who seems to have been an intolerant and irascible person, quarrelled with his protégé, accused him of treachery and put him to death. It may be that Bemoi's enthusiasm for his allies and his new faith had waned as he neared the shores of Guinea, but, whatever the rights and wrongs of this strange incident, a valuable opportunity had been lost.

In the Congo, well beyond the southern limit of Muslim influence, D. João's hope of a Christian ally was at last fulfilled. It will be remembered that the Manicongo had chosen Caçuta as his ambassador and sent him to Portugal with Diogo Cão. In 1489 Gonçalo de Sousa set out with a fleet of three ships to seal the alliance. He had on board not only Caçuta and other Congolese youths – 'now good Christians and fluent in Portuguese' – but also the priests and artisans for whom the Manicongo had asked. But disaster almost overtook this expedition as well. Off Cape Verde both de Sousa and Caçuta died of plague which had been raging in Lisbon when they left; a quarrel over the leadership was only settled by the captain of the island of Santiago in the Cape Verde group.

Eventually they reached their destination under the command of Rui de Sousa, the brother of the dead captain.

If the dates given by Barros[2] are correct, it took them a year to complete the voyage. 'The first part of the Congo they touched was called Sono, where the chief was the King's uncle. When he heard of the arrival of our ships, he was moved by the spirit of God and, accompanied by a crowd of followers, came to meet Rui de Sousa, to the sound of horns, drums and other instruments, as is their custom at times of festival. And through the mouth of one of the young men whom de Sousa had brought with him, he asked to be baptized at once, for he was an old man, and if he must wait while the captain visited the King and returned again, he might die and lose the hope of God's mercy. And when Rui de Sousa saw the urgency of his request, he at once gave orders that the priests should have a great hut built of wood which the servants of the Mani-sono cut. In it three altars were placed, furnished with rich tapestries which had been brought for this sacred purpose. There were present all the sons of the Manisono and all the chiefs of the region, to whom he made a speech, not like a savage, but as one who is moved by the Holy Spirit. And so, on Easter Day 1491, Sono was baptized and given the name of D. Manuel, before more than twenty-five thousand of his people who also offered themselves for baptism.'

Rui de Sousa then set out for the capital at Ambasse. As they approached it, they were met by a guard of warriors who escorted them to the town, singing and beating drums, 'like a religious procession with prayers to the saints. Three or four of them would sing a verse and the whole gathering of people answered them, singing so well that it delighted the Portuguese. From time to time they gave a great shout which seemed to split the heavens and the words of their song were in praise of the King of Portugal and the gifts he had sent to their ruler. The King received them from a wooden platform so high that he could be seen from all sides, sitting on an ebony chair delicately inlaid with ivory in their own style. His upper garments were his own skin, very black and shining, and below he was clothed in a piece of brocade which Diogo Cão had given him. On his left wrist he wore a brass bracelet and on his right shoulder a horse's tail, which is their badge of royalty. On his head was a tall hat, like a mitre, very finely and beautifully woven from palm leaves with patterns like we have on velvet.

'The King put his right hand to the ground and took a handful of dust which he sprinkled on the breast of Rui de Sousa and on his own. There can be no greater courtesy than this. And Rui de Sousa showed the King the appointments which had been brought for his baptism, among them the cross to which the Portuguese made obeisance and the King and his people also.'

These events took place on 29th April. Four days later the foundations of the church were laid. Although stone and lime had to be brought from a distance, it was finished within a month and dedicated to Santa Cruz. It so happened that at this time there was a rebellion among the tribesmen who lived on the islands in the Zaire and the Manicongo had to lead an expedition against them. It was arranged, therefore, that he should be baptized before he left and, on the very day that work on the church was begun, the royal baptism took place before a crowd of a hundred thousand people. In honour of the King of Portugal, he was christened D. João de Congo and his wife took the name of D. Leonor.

It is said that some of the Portuguese fought with the Manicongo against his rebellious subjects. With their help and under a banner emblazoned with a cross, the King won a resounding victory. When he returned, it was time for Rui de Sousa to say good-bye. He left behind the

Dominican, Fr. Antonio, and four other brothers, together with laymen who, with the help of native guides, were to explore the interior of this great kingdom and they, adds Barros[3], 'passed beyond the great lake of which we spoke'.

This reference has been taken to mean that during this period the Portuguese explored the basin of the Congo and even the great lakes of east-central Africa. But this seems very unlikely. Even a hundred years later, when Pigafeta recorded the adventures of Duarte Lopes, it seems far from certain that the great lakes had actually been reached. On the map with which Pigafeta's book is illustrated, there appears Lake Aquilinda, on the marshy plateau from which flow the Kasai, several tributaries of the Zambezi and shorter rivers which flow into the Atlantic south of the Congo. It may be that five hundred years ago this upland region was even wetter, sufficiently so to justify the name of a Great Lake.

The conversion of the kingdom of the Congo did not go unopposed. Barros[4] records what happened in the capital, newly renamed S. Salvador, after the departure of Rui de Sousa. 'On his return from the frontiers, the son of D. João de Congo was baptized with many of the nobles who had gone with him and for love of D. Afonso, Prince of Portugal, he took the same name. But with the baptism every day of so many people, the Devil was losing his power and must needs strive to hold in pawn some person of royal birth through whom he could redeem his losses. Now there was another son of the King, called Panso Aquitimo, who did not wish to be baptized and who collected round him some of those who were in agreement with his views.

'The King himself also grew discontented because the priests wished him to put aside the many women he had and keep only one, as the Church commanded. And these women, because of the precepts of the priests, were like to lose their status as royal wives and they made common cause with the wives of the King's intimates and plotted with their husbands to persuade the King not to agree to what had been demanded. And because the King was an old man, he listened to the advice of his friends and inclined once more to the ancient customs.

'The Prince Afonso, in whom belief in the Faith was stronger, defended what he had confessed with all his power. But his enemies began to stir up the King to indignation against his son, until he was dismissed from favour and the pagan Panso installed in his place. Because all the people of this part of Ethiopia were much given to sorcery, the ministers of the Devil said to the King that he must know that his son D. Afonso, from the limits of the kingdom where he then was, by means of the arts which the Christians had taught him, came flying every night and entered in upon those women, that is, those who had been kept from the King by order of the priests, and had intercourse with them and thereafter returned whence he had come. In addition to this injury, they said, the Prince had learnt how to dry up rivers and bring other evils on the land, so that the King drew less tribute from his realm than heretofore and had less to give to those who served him faithfully. On the other hand, the King was advised by those chiefs who were friends of the Prince that all these things were untrue, inasmuch as his son was to be seen in the region where he was both by day and by night. In order to make better sure of the truth about the Prince, the King sent a fetish wrapped in a cloth to a woman of whose virtue he was suspicious and told the boy who carried it to her to

say that D. Afonso had sent it, in order to free himself from
the sentence of death to which the King had condemned
him. But the woman, being innocent of offence, told the
youth to put the fetish on the floor and went to tell the
King of the offering she had received from his son and of
other matters by which the King knew her innocence and
agreed with those who told him that the Prince had been
maligned. A few days later, without giving an account of
this affair to anyone, he sent for his son and restored to him
all his lands and honours. To add to the confusion of the
enemies of the Prince, he ordered them to be put to
death. . . .'

Soon afterwards the King fell ill. His son Panso took up
his position close to the capital so that he could seize it if
the King should die. But D. Afonso also lay close to the
city, '. . . and when the King's death was confirmed, he was
advised by the Queen his mother to enter into it secretly
and silently by night and that, whoever should come in his
company, should come a few at a time with baskets on
their heads in which their weapons were hidden, saying
that they were bringing provisions for her. Having entered
in this way, the next day the Prince appeared on the terrace
of the palace and was proclaimed King with a great noise
of shouting and beating of drums as was their custom. So
great was the noise that it carried to the camp outside the
city where Panso was only waiting for more of his followers
to make himself King by force of arms. Hearing that his
brother had only a small company to defend him, Panso at
once began to enter the city. The King had only thirty-seven
Christians with him, but, like a man well-versed in the arts
of war and commanded by God, he told his men to await
the coming of the Prince Panso in the great square, for he
relied on the mercy of God to bring him victory over his
enemies. And this trust failed him not, for when the first

of their companies entered the square, there fell on them a great rain of arrows which was a miraculous event. And the King's men stayed not from calling on the name of God and of the apostle St. James until his brother's men turned their backs and fled in to the ranks of the second company, whom also they put to flight. With the help of God, the victory of the Catholic King was complete and his brother fled into the bush, where he fell into a pit prepared for wild animals and there was captured together with his principal captain.

'Now this captain besought the King that he might allow him to be baptized before he died. For he now believed in the God whom all men adore, because, at the time of their attack, he had seen a host of armed men on horseback beneath the banner of the Christians and this was the cause of their defeat. The King, believing in his penitence, not only ordered his prayer to be granted, but spared his life. In memory of this happening, he and all his family were ordered to sweep and clean the church and bring water with which the pagans might be baptized.

'As for Panso, he was so badly injured by his fall into the game-pit and by the downfall of his cause, that he died. And the King brought peace to his kingdom and reigned for fifty years.'

In 1487 D. João decided to try a more direct approach to the Empire of Prester John. It is surprising that the Portuguese had made no such attempt before. For though the remote mountains and gorges of the kingdom they sought lay behind the curtain of Muslim principalities in the valley of the Nile and on the shores of the Red Sea, it was not entirely cut off from the western world. Monks from Ethiopia were in the habit of visiting Jerusalem from time to time; since St. Frumentius had converted the people to Christianity in the fourth century A.D., the Abuna, the Head of the Ethiopian Church, had been appointed by the Patriarch of Alexandria; no doubt these Abunas had long and difficult journeys to reach their See and some failed to arrive at all, yet apparently the succession of Egyptian bishops had been maintained. Moreover, there are many references in fifteenth-century chronicles to visits by 'embassies' from Ethiopia to various parts of Europe. In 1402 envoys from the Emperor were received at Venice; in 1427 a similar mission visited the kingdom of Aragon shortly before D. Pedro of Portugal arrived there on his way home from his travels. In 1441 and again in 1450 priests from Ethiopia reached Rome and were received in audience by the Pope. In 1459 Ethiopian ambassadors presented themselves to the Duke of Milan.

The visits to the Pope are particularly interesting. In the fifth century the Coptic Church of Ethiopia, like the Alexandrine Church from which it stemmed, had adopted the Monophysite heresy. It held that there is but one nature in the person of Christ in opposition to the orthodox doctrine that Christ has two natures, the human and the divine. But Zara Jacob, who ascended the throne of the Lion of Judah in 1439, finding, like most Emperors before and since, that the Coptic Church was a millstone round his neck, decided to transfer his allegiance to Rome. His approaches came to nothing, but from the middle of the century much of the fog of mystery which surrounded his empire must have begun to dissolve.

There are records also of missions dispatched to Ethiopia from France, Aragon and Rome itself in the person of the friar Baptista de Imola. But there is no evidence to show that any of these travellers reached their destination or, if they did, that they ever returned. As will be seen, such few foreigners as succeeded in struggling up the mountain passes to the court of Prester John were kept there until they died.

By 1487 D. João had already made one attempt to reach Ethiopia by way of Egypt. He had sent two priests, but they, travelling openly as envoys of the King of Portugal, were unable to go further than Jerusalem. He then chose two men of a very different stamp, Pêro de Covilhã and Afonso de Paiva, hardy villagers from the eastern slopes of the Serra de Estrêla. Little is known of Afonso's previous life, but Pêro de Covilhã had behind him a long and adventurous career. He spoke Arabic fluently and had plenty of experience of Muslim customs.

With the King's blessing and a grant of two hundred *cruzados,* they set out for Alexandria by way of Barcelona and Rhodes[5]. In Alexandria they disguised themselves as Arab merchants and, in the company of a party of Moors from the Maghreb, they succeeded in reaching Aden. Here they separated. Afonso de Paiva eventually died in Cairo, but nothing is known of his wanderings. Pêro de Covilhã embarked on a dhow for India. Few details of his astonishing journeys over the next few years have survived, but enough is known to show that the first Portuguese traveller in the East was not a man to waste his time. He spent over a year in India: at the ports of Cananor, Calicut and Goa he was able to see for himself the legendary wealth of the Indies. He examined the trade in spices, the pepper and ginger which commanded so high a price in the markets of Europe; he was shown the gold and precious stones with which the palaces and even the warehouses of these cities abounded. When he had seen all there was to see, and made notes for his royal master, he departed for Ormuz, the great trading port at the mouth of the Persian Gulf. At Ormuz, as the monsoon was favourable, he

embarked on a dhow southward bound for Sofala, far to
the south of the Equator on the east cost of Africa. Here
the Arab merchants collected the gold which had been
mined in the far interior of the continent and Covilhã was
able to add the details of this trade to his growing store of
knowledge. From Sofala he sailed for Aden once more
and eventually arrived in Cairo. He had been away from
home for nearly five years and he must have hoped that the
time had now come for him to return to his family in
Portugal.

But in Cairo two Jews, agents of D. João, were waiting
for him with letters from the King. 'If you have fulfilled all
your original instructions', he was told, 'you can come home.
But if you have not yet reached the kingdom of Prester
John, then you must do so to complete the assignment you
have been given.' D. João asked a great deal of those who
served him. So, one would suppose, with a heavy heart,
Pêro de Covilhã sat down in Cairo to write a full report of
his journeys, including, no doubt, a map to show the
places he had visited. He sent it to his master by the hand
of Mestre Joseph, the shoemaker of Lamego. We do not
know what was in his report, but if he gave an accurate
account of all he had seen and done, it must have been one
of the most valuable documents in the King's archives.
D. João and his advisers would have studied it carefully
and a few years later Vasco da Gama would also have made
good use of the information it contained.

In accordance with the further instructions of D. João,
Covilhã left Cairo once more to escort the other Jew, the
Rabbi Abraham, to Aden and Ormuz. This task completed,
in 1490 he turned his attention at last to Ethiopia. He is
said to have landed at Zeilah, a little port on the northern
coast of what is now the Republic of Somalia. He still had
in front of him a long and arduous journey before he reached

the Court of Prester John in the neighbourhood of Lake Dambea (Lake Tana). One would like to know whether he followed the more direct route across the savage desert where the Danakil now live and up the precipitous escarpment beyond or whether he travelled by the ancient city of Harar and the uplands of Shoa. But on this, as on so many other interesting details, the chronicles are silent.

We know, however, that the Emperor Iskander (Alexander), was quick to welcome his unusual guest and was greatly pleased with the letters from his fellow-monarch in Portugal. He began the long-drawn-out task of preparing a suitable answer. But then, suddenly, he died. His brother Naod, who succeeded him, was not interested in the prospect of an alliance with his Christian colleague. Moreover, he said, it was not the custom to allow foreigners to leave the country. Pêro de Covilhã must stay where he was.

He was not ill treated; he was given land and a handsome bride, by whom he had several sons. In 1521, when the embassy of D. Roderigo de Lima reached Ethiopia, he was still alive, but too old to undertake the journey home to Portugal. So D. João waited in vain for his return. As Rui de Pina says, 'Nothing is known of what he finally achieved, for he never came back from his travels[6].'

The Treaty of Tordesillas

In spite of his preoccupations overseas, D. João had never lost sight of his desire to bring about the union of Portugal with the kingdoms of Castile and Aragon. Since the experiences of his father had convinced him that his ambitions could not be achieved by force, they must, therefore, be realized by peaceful means. In 1483, when the *terçarias* had been dissolved, it had been agreed that when D. Afonso of Portugal, D. João's only legitimate child, reached the age of fourteen, he should marry Juana, the second daughter of *Los Reyes Católicos*. If by then, however, their eldest daughter, the Infanta Isabella, was still unmarried, D. Afonso should marry her instead. In 1488, when the Prince was thirteen, D. Isabella was still unbetrothed.

Whatever may have been the feelings of their subjects, this marriage was ardently desired by the parents of both children. But it would never do to show too much eagerness and both sides settled down to a contest in diplomatic gamesmanship. Ferdinand and Isabella made the opening ploy: rumours were allowed to circulate that negotiations had been opened for the betrothal of the Princess to the Dauphin, the son of Louis XI of France. When this gambit seemed played out, it was reported that the heir to the throne of Naples was to be the lucky man. Though well aware that these tales had been put about for his benefit, D. João responded with a period of intense activity on his frontiers. Fortresses which had been allowed to fall into disrepair since the Treaty of Alcaçovas were refurbished and their garrisons brought up to strength.

As D. João well knew, a threat from Portugal at this moment would have been inconvenient and embarrassing to Castile. Ferdinand and Isabella were engaged in a war of attrition in Granada. Their armies were gradually closing in on the heart of the Moorish kingdom, but, in the difficult country which surrounded its capital, their operations were a laborious and costly business which were absorbing all their attention and resources. They made haste to enquire what designs D. João had on them and to assure him of their everlasting friendship and cousinly affection. In private D. João had already consulted his advisers and obtained their support for the proposed marriage. But he made no public move throughout 1489 and it was only in January 1490 that he at last summoned the Cortes and put the suggestion to them. It was greeted with acclamation and the unprecedented sum of 100,000 *cruzados* was voted to cover the cost of it. It was only then, with the Prince in his sixteenth year, that the King dispatched ambassadors to Seville to make a formal request on behalf of his son for the hand of the Princess.

The embassy was led by Fernão da Silveira, the Master of the Horse. It was enthusiastically received, Rui de Pina tells us, as no embassy had been received in Spain before. Well might Ferdinand and Isabella be pleased, for it seemed that at last the threat of *La Beltreneja* was about to be finally laid. They examined a portrait of D. Afonso, tinted *au naturel,* which the ambassadors had brought with them. D. Isabella, who had last seen her bridegroom-to-be at Moura at the age of eight, was entranced. The Prince was a good-looking boy, with fair hair and 'English' colouring. But it should perhaps be noted that the chroniclers hint that

D. João himself was not so entranced with his son and found him a trifle effeminate for his taste.

With Fernão da Silveira representing the bridegroom, the proxy wedding of the two royal children took place at Seville on the Sunday after Easter 1490. The festivities lasted all night and meanwhile relays of squires on horseback carried the news to Évora, where the King awaited it with mounting excitement. When at last the dispatches arrived, the city went mad with joy: the bells pealed; trumpets sounded; bombards were fired; torches were lit; the streets decorated with foliage and banners unfurled on all the walls, towers and prominent landmarks in sight of the town. With the King at this great moment were the Queen and her only surviving brother, D. Manuel, Duke of Beja. Since the King had executed the Duke of Viseu and proclaimed D. Manuel next in succession to the throne after his own son, 'the Duke' had been in constant attendance at Court. But though often mentioned, his personality makes hardly a scratch on the chronicles of the reign, as he follows, a silent, self-effacing figure, in the footsteps of his royal uncle.

The immediate rejoicings after the ceremony at Seville were cut short by the death of the King's sister, D. Joana. Although she had persistently frustrated her brother's hopes for a 'useful' marriage and had retired into a nunnery against his wishes, D. João had been very fond of her. But he did not allow his regret to interfere with his plans for making his son's wedding one which none of those who attended it would ever forget. The King as a rule was careful with his money, but, where the prestige of his family and his kingdom were concerned, he was not going to count his pennies. The arrangements were in charge of D. Martinho de Castelo Branco who worked in an office in the palace under his master's eye. For the festivities, which were to include balls, banquets, mimes, concerts and jousting, the King ordered all manner of equipment to be collected, brocades, silks and tapestries for decorating the walls; wax for the candles; game, fish, spices, fruit and preserves; horses, saddlery, lances and other trappings for the tournaments. He summoned all the prelates, nobles and knights to the wedding and asked them to bring with them the furnishings of their houses, especially beds and tables of which there was a great shortage at Évora. Because many of the *fidalgos* were poor, the King agreed to give them credit to be repaid over two years, or to lend them silks and jewellery, woollen cloaks, dinner services of silver and even horses and slaves.

Farmers from all over Portugal were asked to bring fowls, capons, ducks and birds of all kinds; wheat, barley, flour, cattle and sheep; the local peasants must organize herds of cows and goats to supply milk to the town; hunters must bring in game and fishermen their catches and this they must continue to do until the entertainments were at an end. Every artificer and craftsman in the kingdom was set to work and, because there were not enough to do all that was needed, others were brought from overseas, jewellers, goldsmiths, enamellers, weavers and leather-workers as well as cooks and minstrels. The countries of Europe and northern Africa were combed for their wealth; silks and brocades, precious stones, tapestries, carpets, woollen cloth, silver, even ermine and other furs, were bought from Flanders, England, Ireland, Germany and the merchant cities of Italy; wax from Barbary, green and dried fruit, preserves, honey, butter and spices. Moors were summoned who could sing, dance or play musical instruments and from all over Portugal pretty girls were brought to entertain the guests.

The King had chosen Évora for the official wedding

service and for the festivities surrounding it because the plague was endemic in Lisbon and because it lay conveniently close to the frontier with Castile. But although it was then the second city of Portugal, there was nowhere in it large enough to hold the multitude who were expected. So a banquet hall was built of wood in the grounds of the monastery of St. Francis. It was more than a hundred feet long, fifty feet wide and, according to Rui de Pina, nearly fifty feet high. The walls were hung with tapestries and draperies; there was a dais at one end for the royal party; against the farther wall there were four smaller platforms for the minstrels and other entertainers; there were seven long tables down each side for the guests with a wide aisle of smooth stone between them; overhead were twenty candelabra of painted wood, each to hold four candles, and each fitted with a basin so that the wax should not drip into the dishes as they were carried in by an army of servants.

During the warm days of the late summer, when the preparations were almost complete and every corner of the city was already crowded, the plague appeared in Évora. On the advice of his doctors, the King ordered the town and all the countryside around it to be evacuated for a fortnight, so that it was left to the herds of cattle and the handful of Alentejan herdsmen who looked after them. This drastic remedy seems to have been effective and, by the end of October, D. João was able to tell Ferdinand and Isabella that he was ready to receive their daughter.

On 22nd November the Princess reached the frontier. She was welcomed in the name of the King by the Duke of Beja and a glittering cavalcade of noblemen who escorted her to Estremoz. Here the King and his son, who could not wait to meet his bride, paid an unexpected call on her. The state entry into Évora and the ceremony in the cathedral were planned for the following Sunday, but the King arranged for the Archbishop of Braga to bless the union privately at Estremoz. It was rumoured that the Prince, who had at once fallen deeply in love with D. Isabella, did not wait for the blessing of the church and spent the night with her at Estremoz, thereby greatly scandalizing the good monks of the monastery of Santa Maria where she was staying.

The festivities were all that the King had planned. They began with a ball on the night of the bride's arrival and continued throughout the following week. At the banquet table, at the masques and in the arena, D. João outshone all his guests. After the jousting the judges awarded him the prizes, a diamond ring for his accoutrements and a collar of gold for his skill in the tourneys. 'This', says Rui de Pina, 'was no unjust award[1].'

At the end of the week the company began quickly to disperse, for the plague was once more beginning to threaten the city. The revels were over and it was time to go home. As it turned out, the wedding of his son was the climax of D. João's reign. He was still a young man, only in his mid-thirties, and might well have thought that he had many years of life in front of him. Yet he had only five, for immediately after the wedding the first signs of the sickness which killed him made their appearance. This would, perhaps, not have distressed him overmuch, if his plans for the future union of Portugal and Castile had not gone so sadly awry. In the following July, his son and heir, D. Afonso, riding beside the river at Santarém, stumbled and fell from his horse on to his head. He was carried to a near-by hut, the home of a poor fisherman and there, many hours later, he died without recovering consciousness.

Some time in 1484 Christopher Columbus had come to lay before D. João his proposals for reaching the islands of Cipangu by sailing westward across the Atlantic Ocean. This strange man had first arrived in Portugal quite by chance. According to one story, the ship in which he was travelling from his native Genoa was sunk by a French squadron off the Algarve and he swam ashore near Lagos. His younger brother was already living in Lisbon, where he had set himself up as a chart-maker. Columbus joined him and went into partnership with him. He married the daughter of Bartolemeu Perestrello, he who had introduced the rabbits into the island of Porto Santo.

This is not the place to probe the mysteries of Columbus' early career, nor to consider how the son of a Genoese weaver, if that is what he was, came to marry into the Portuguese aristocracy, to have the ear of kings, and to treat with master-mariners on their own ground. But it appears that his mother-in-law gave him some of her late husband's papers and from these he may have learnt of the existence of land to the west of the Açores. He would have picked up his very considerable knowledge of navigation from his brother the chart-maker and from his wife's step-brother, who had inherited the captaincy of Porto Santo. He seems to have taken part in at least one voyage to the new fortress at Elmina and also to have visited Madeira and other Atlantic islands.

All these things helped to make Columbus an accomplished seaman. But they did not account for his conviction that God had chosen him for a great enterprise, nor for his unyielding singleness of purpose, nor for his presumption in insisting on his own conditions. He would, he told the King, acquire for the Crown of Portugal vast new territories and unimaginable wealth, but the King must find and equip for him three caravels to sail under his own command; he must appoint him Admiral of the Ocean Sea; he must grant him the hereditary title of Viceroy of all the lands he might discover and he must award him a tenth of the profits of his ventures.

These conditions shocked D. João and his advisers. Nevertheless, his plans, even though they had been put forward by a foreign upstart, had to be studied very carefully. The King had set up a committee to consider all matters concerned with overseas exploration. It included such expert cartographers, geographers and mathematicians as his chaplain, D. Diogo Ortiz, his doctor, Roderigo the Jew, Joseph Vizinho and D. Duarte Pacheco, the future author of *Esmeraldo do Situ Orbis*. It may also have included Martin Behaim, the German scholar who constructed the oldest globe which is still in existence. No doubt captains such as Diogo Cão, if he was still alive, and Bartolemeu Dias, were called in for consultation. Over Columbus' schemes they must have deliberated long and anxiously. It has been suggested that the King was inclined to believe in them, but that the committee of experts overruled him and so lost to Portugal a wonderful opportunity. But it does not seem likely that a man who had negotiated the Treaty of Alcaçovas and steered his way through the conspiracies of the Braganças and of the Duke of Viseu would have accepted his counsellors' advice unless he had cogent reasons for so doing.

Even if we assume that D. João was ignorant of the voyages of the Norsemen in the eleventh century and even if we regard as apocryphal the visit of João Vaz de Corte Real to 'the land of codfish' in 1474, there was still a good deal of evidence for the existence of the lands in which Columbus believed. Various objects of unknown origin had been washed up on the shores of the Açores; captains blown off their course on their way home from Guinea by the Atlantic route had reported sighting land far to the west and a title to any lands he might discover 'beyond the parts of Guinea' had been granted to Fernão Teles in 1474. It is possible that the mainland coast of South America had already been reached. The question which the Portuguese had to decide was not so much whether lands existed in the far west, but whether they could be, as Columbus claimed, the islands of Cipangu or dependencies of the Indies. That the earth was round was no longer in dispute, at least among learned men. But the length of the circumference of the earth and the eastward extent of the continent of Asia were still the subject of vehement argument.

The length of a degree of longitude at the Equator is slightly over 69 miles; the circumference of the earth is, therefore, 24,860 miles. The fact that the meridians of longitude run closer together as they approach the Poles was only mistily understood by fifteenth-century cartographers, who had, in any case, no way of calculating accurately their exact position. The values for a degree of longitude used by the makers of maps and charts varied greatly, but they often used the distance true for about 40°N, the approximate latitude of Lisbon, the central Mediterranean, southern Italy and northern Greece. This was about 56 miles. Such an error was enough in itself to reduce the circumference of the earth by more than 4,000 miles and so bring the supposed position of eastern Asia that much closer to Europe[2].

In addition, the dimensions of Asia from west to east were often greatly exaggerated. The Ptolemaic idea of a land-locked Indian Ocean had now been abandoned and the journeyings of Nicolo Conti had filled in many of the details of the map of Asia. But cartographers were still influenced by the earlier travels of Marco Polo, who had much overestimated the length of his journey to the palace of the Great Khan, by the *Imago Mundi* of Cardinal D'Ailly, and by the 7,548 islands of eastern Asia which appeared in the Catalan Atlas. Although in Fra Mauro's map of 1459 the eastward extent of Asia had been much reduced, it does not appear that the celebrated Toscanelli altogether agreed with him. A combination of the reduced degree of longitude, an increase in the width of the Asian continent and the judicious use of islands would bring the Indies within reasonable reach of Europe by the western route. All these misconceptions were incorporated by Martin Behaim on the globe which he constructed during the fourteen-nineties.

Columbus predicted an ocean crossing of about 2,500 miles. Against the variable winds in the latitude of the Açores, this might have proved a formidable task. But he proposed to make use of the trade winds which, nearer the Equator, blew steadily from the north-east. He based his calculations on various travellers' tales, on quotations from the book of Esdras[3] and on a letter written by Toscanelli in 1474 to encourage the King of Portugal to seek his objective by sailing westward. This letter, which has been declared to be a forgery and even attributed to Columbus himself, asserted that the total distance from Lisbon to the city of Cathay was 6,500 miles, but that the crossing from the island of Antilia, the existence of which is taken for granted, was only 2,500 miles.

Since no map or chart from Portuguese sources has survived from this period, we cannot be certain what D. João and his committee thought. But it seems probable from the Cantino map of 1502 that they were aware of the greater length of a degree of longitude at the Equator, although they may not have been able to calculate it exactly. They also seem to have suspected that the width of Asia

ad been exaggerated by many geographers. They would
herefore have decided that, even if Columbus found land
vhere he expected it to be, he would still be a great distance
rom the mainland of Asia and that it was far more likely
hat he would sail away into the Atlantic and never be
heard of again.

D. João had other reasons for rejecting Columbus. He
and his predecessors had invested a great deal of money
n the African route and Diogo Cão had recently returned
rom his first voyage with news which suggested that
success was near. The King could not afford to dissipate
his resources, nor could he expect much help from the
nobles and merchants for such a dubious scheme. Nor did
he wish to employ such an unlikable foreigner when he
had so many competent navigators of his own.

By way of insurance, in 1484 he offered to Fernão
Domingues the captaincy of an island 'which he is now
setting out to seek'[4] and two years later made a similar
offer to Fernão Dulmo and João Afonso do Estreito[5]. This
grant specifically mentions the Island of the Seven Cities
The two men were to share the expenses and to sail from
Terceira in the Açores within a year. Fernão Dulmo was
to set the course for the first forty days and, if by that time
no islands or terra firma had been discovered, the choice of
course was to go to his partner.

There is no evidence that any of these captains ever took
up the challenge. Indeed, the prevailing westerlies in the
latitude of the Açores made the islands a poor starting
point for voyages into the Atlantic. But meanwhile D.
João's answer to Columbus was No, and the Genoese left
Portugal hurriedly and in debt to begin his long siege of
Ferdinand and Isabella in Castile.

Los Reyes Católicos had other things on their minds.
Once their hold on their dual kingdom had been firmly

established, they set about the task of uniting the whole Iberian peninsula into a single Christian realm. Their plans for a dynastic union with Portugal were only one aspect of this policy, which included also the disinfection of their own subjects from non-Christian influences. In 1480 they introduced the Inquisition, an organization for the prevention of doctrinal irregularities among those who called themselves Christians. They then began to prepare for an assault on Granada, the kingdom in the south which had been under Muslim rule for more than seven centuries. Although they were greatly helped by internal dissensions among the Moors, their long campaign only ended on 2nd January 1492 with the triumphal entry of their forces into the city of Granada itself. Two months later the decree was signed which ordered the expulsion of the Jews. This uncharitable act was financially very profitable to the Crown, since the unfortunate victims, estimated at more than 150,000, were allowed to take with them only what they could carry and the export of gold and silver was forbidden.

With their kingdoms so cleansed, Ferdinand and Isabella were able to turn their attention to Columbus, who had been pestering them on and off for years. For much of this time he had been living on charity at the Franciscan Monastery of La Rabida near the mouth of the Rio Tinto and it was from this house, in the shabby clothes which were all he then possessed, that he hastened to obey the royal summons.

Throughout his negotiations in Castile, Columbus had obstinately insisted on the same conditions he had put forward to D. João of Portugal. He wanted three ships under his own command for the voyage, the titles of Admiral of the Ocean and Viceroy of such lands as he might discover and one tenth of the revenues from them.

urrounded as they were by *hidalgos* of the bluest blood, erdinand and Isabella cannot have appreciated these condiions any more than had D. João. Nevertheless, they ecided to back him. It is not clear exactly why they did o. Although both Castile and Aragon had behind them a ong maritime tradition, the geographical expertise of the ourteenth century had been largely lost and they could all upon none of the informed advice which was available n Portugal. A special commission, set up to examine the roposals, had advised the Queen to have no part in them. ut Columbus was a compulsive talker and he was suported by the Prior of La Rabida, Father Juan Perez, who ad once been the Queen's confessor. It may be that it eemed a reasonable gamble. The town of Palos had reently been fined two ships for some misdemeanour and hese could be allocated to the expedition. Ferdinand's Treasurer, Luiz de Santangel, offered to cover the cost of equipment, stores and wages. The chances were, of course, hat neither Columbus nor his crews would ever be heard of again, but if he should happen to be successful, Ferdinand and Isabella would stand to gain immense wealth and prestige in return for a very small investment. No doubt, if it ever became necessary, the lawyers could deal with the preposterous claims of Columbus and his family.

Dressed now as befitted his station, the new Admiral returned to the Rio Tinto. The municipality of Palos reluctantly produced two rather elderly ships and Columbus was able to charter for his flagship the *Santa Maria* of Juan de la Cosa which happened to be in the port. With perseverance and ingenuity, he overcame all the obstacles and objections which were put in his way, but had it not been for the help of the Pinzon family, he might never have been able to man his ships. He sailed from Palos on 3rd August 1492.

On 4th March 1493, to the consternation of some and the astonishment of almost everyone, Columbus reappeared and sailed into the Tagus. He brought with him a few gold ornaments, many tales of marvels he had seen or thought he ought to have seen and a group of black-haired, near naked, brown-skinned 'Indians' who shivered unhappily in the chill of a Portuguese winter. He had accomplished one of the most notable feats in the history of the world and he had reached the threshold of a new continent, but he was convinced, and remained convinced, throughout three more voyages and to the end of his life, that the islands he had discovered were off the coasts of Asia and that the riches of the Indies were as good as his for the taking. He was a little above himself. Invited to the Portuguese Court, he patronized D. João and rallied him on letting slip the opportunity which had been offered to him nearly ten years before. The King questioned him narrowly he could see for himself that the 'Indians' resembled no Africans he had ever seen, but he was concerned to make sure that his visitor had not trespassed on his preserves in Guinea. He did not think it likely that these scared and ignorant savages could have come from India or Cipangu or Cathay if the stories he had heard about the wealth and culture of these countries were in any way true. There remained the bare possibility that Columbus was right and that he had indeed reached some outlying frontier of the continent of Asia.

What, then, was to be done? Some, who were not in the King's confidence, suggested that Columbus should be quietly disposed of before he could make his report to Castile and that Ferdinand and Isabella should be told that he had died of plague in Lisbon. But D. João, after long discussions with his advisers and, no doubt, a careful reappraisement of all the knowledge at their disposal, decided that whatever the islands might be which Columbus had discovered, they were still a very great distance from Asia and that the Castilians should be encouraged rather than hindered from persevering with their adventures in the western ocean. He treated Columbus with respect and sent him on his way to Castile.

Ferdinand and Isabella greeted the Admiral warmly. But, if they were to profit by his exploits, there was no time to be lost. A rumour had already reached them that D. João of Portugal was convinced that the islands which Columbus had discovered belonged to him and that he was already preparing a fleet to take possession of them. They therefore at once set in motion plans for a second and larger expedition which would, among other things, establish a permanent trading post on the island of Hispaniola. Meanwhile they instructed Columbus to write a report of his voyage to the Pope, proving that the islands he had found were beyond the regions which had previously been assigned to Portugal. It was standard practice at this time to obtain the mandate of the Papacy in respect of newly-discovered lands, since, in theory at any rate, the most important consequence was the conversion of the inhabitants to Christianity.

As it happened, Pope Alexander VI was of Spanish descent, being the second and most notorious member of the Borgia family to hold the office. He owed his election in the previous year largely to the support of Ferdinand and Isabella and was, on that account, willing to grant them whatever they asked. He endorsed the Spanish claims in a series of Bulls, of which the best known, that of 4th May 1493, divided the world into two parts by a line drawn from north to south one hundred leagues west of the Açores; all lands newly-discovered or to be discovered to the east of this line were to belong to Portugal and all those to the west of it to Spain.

The King of Portugal did not accept this ruling. He at once opened the negotiations with Ferdinand and Isabella which resulted in the Treaty of Tordesillas of 1494. By this agreement, Pope Alexander's line was moved, to 370 leagues west of the Cape Verde Islands, that is from about 34°W to about 48°W. In order to understand why D. João should insist on this modification it is necessary to consider what he might have been doing since the return of Bartolemeu Dias in 1488. The chronicles are silent: there is in them no mention of any voyage of exploration under the Portuguese flag between 1488 and the summer of 1497 when Vasco da Gama set out on his successful voyage to India by way of southern Africa. By that time D. João had been dead for eighteen months. But it is inconceivable that, in the seven years of life which still remained to him, he should have done nothing to make sure of the prize which had been brought so nearly within his grasp.

The solution to this mystery can surely be found in the ships which Gama commanded and the course which he was ordered to follow across the Atlantic. The *naos* of Gama's fleet were quite different from the caravels which had served his predecessors so well and must have taken several years to develop and build. Though slower, perhaps, and less handy than the caravels, they were larger and heavier, more suitable for long ocean passages and with more room for stores; they were rigged square rather than fore-and-aft and were strengthened so that they could carry rudimentary cannon. The only clue we have to experiments on this type of vessel is the appearance of the *Rainha*, which D. João named after his Queen and allocated to the Mediterranean trade.

But the route which Gama followed is even more revealing. It will be remembered that the earlier explorers had hugged the coast of Africa on their outward voyages, taking on stores at the fort of S. Jorge da Mina and battling against the adverse winds and currents off the west coast of southern Africa. It was only when Dias sailed boldly out into the Atlantic to pick up the variable winds in higher latitudes that he was able to turn the Cape of Good Hope. Vasco da Gama did not hug the coast. He called at the Cape Verde Islands and thereafter was sixty-two days out of sight of land. Details of his voyage are scanty, but the most satisfactory reconstruction suggests that from the Cape Verde Islands he first headed south-east until, off Sierra Leone, he parted company with Bartolemeu Dias who was on his way to take up his appointment as Governor of the fortress of S. Jorge. Gama then set a course south by west until, in a latitude of about 30°S, he picked up a favourable westerly wind to carry him back to Africa. In so doing he blazed a trail which was to be followed for the next four hundred years by pilots of all nationalities. This cannot have been mere chance. It suggests a close study of the winds and currents of the south Atlantic over a period of years. A glance at the map will show that if this was indeed the course he followed, he must have passed very close to the coast of South America where the modern Brazilian province of Pernambuco bulges into the ocean a few degrees south of the Equator. If D. João's captains had already investigated this area, they must have sighted land; it would have been extraordinary if they had not. Whether they realized that what they had seen was terra firma or whether they imagined it to be a chain of islands, there is no means of telling.

Brazil, called originally Vera Cruz, the 'Land of the True Cross', was officially 'discovered' in 1500 by Pedro Álvares Cabral, the Captain-General of the second fleet dispatched to India by D. Manuel. His discoveries were reported to the King in such matter-of-fact terms that one may be forgiven for supposing that he already knew what the letter was likely to contain[6]. It has been suggested that Dias himself might have been the first to sight Vera Cruz; others have attributed this exploit to Pêro Vaz da Cunha, the bad-tempered captain who had so summarily put the Christian chief Bemoi to death. One wonders whether his voyage, which has been assigned to 1489, was in the nature of a punishment. Other records from early settlers in Brazil claim that by 1530 the country had already been known to the Portuguese, and indeed colonized by them, for more than forty years.

D. João liked to keep to himself as much of the detail of his discoveries as he could and this policy would have applied not only to Vera Cruz itself, if indeed it had been reached, but also to the course which a ship must follow in order to reach South Africa. It could, therefore, be argued that he wished to redraw Pope Alexander's line in order to ensure that his captains, on their way to the Cape of Good Hope, could sail unmolested by the Spaniards, but much the most satisfactory explanation of his conduct is that he already knew that there was land across the Atlantic in the southern hemisphere; that, whether it was islands or terra firma, it was suitable for colonization and that it was to be found in the neighbourhood of 36°W.

Tordesillas is a small village on the plateau of high Castile where in the following century the unfortunate Queen Juana, known as the 'Mad', was to be imprisoned in a convent for much of her life. Here the King's Proctors, Rui de Sousa, Aires de Almada and their secretary, Estevão Vaz, settled down to carry out their master's instructions. The Treaty was finally signed in September 1494[7]. It ratified, first of all, the Treaty of Alcaçovas, confirming that Granada nd the Canaries belonged to Spain and that D. João was King of the Algarves, both 'here and beyond the sea' – that is, of his North African possessions – and Lord of Guinea. It then established, as D. João wished, a line of demarcation between the Spanish and the Portuguese 'spheres of influence' drawn from Pole to Pole 370 leagues west of the Cape Verde Islands. All islands and continents, already discovered or to be discovered, were to belong to the respective monarchs and their heirs for ever.

It was further agreed that within ten months after the signing of the treaty two or four caravels, one or two from each side, were to meet in the Canaries. They were to have on board pilots, astrologers [*sic*], mariners and other knowledgeable persons; from the Canaries they were to sail to the Cape Verde Islands and from there westward until they reached the line of demarcation; this they were to follow as far as possible from north to south and, where the line ran across an island or continent, they were to set up towers or other marks of identification on the border.

An interesting proviso followed: it said that, if before the middle of July 1494, any lands were discovered within the most westerly 120 leagues of the Portuguese region, they should belong, nevertheless, to the Spanish Crown. Columbus was at this time absent on his second voyage and had already been away for almost a year; it must be supposed that Ferdinand and Isabella insisted on this clause in case the Admiral brought back news of some fresh discovery, such as Antilia, which was not as far west as the agreed line of demarcation. One can imagine the wrangling that this particular paragraph must have caused.

Finally, the ambassadors, both of Spain and Portugal, swore on the wood of the true cross that they and their principals would abide by the Treaty and loyally observe its conditions.

D. João had got what he wanted. He could now take legal possession of Vera Cruz and his ships could sail unhindered in the south Atlantic. But the arrangements for determining the exact position of the line of demarcation were never carried out. Indeed, it is doubtful whether, with the nautical expertise available at the time, they ever could have been. But this omission does not seem to have led to any immediate controversy. The Portuguese were nibbling at Brazil from its eastern coast: Columbus was occupied far to the north and west and the *conquistadores* were soon to become much more interested in Mexico, Panama and Peru than in Atlantic islands. It was only thirty-odd years later, when the Portuguese had reached the archipelago which we now call Indonesia from the west and Magellan, a Portuguese in the service of Spain, had approached these same islands from the opposite direction, that any serious difference of opinion arose. By that time the line agreed upon at Tordesillas was generally held to circumscribe the globe and therefore to run from Pole to Pole in the eastern hemisphere as well as in the west. The exact position of the valuable Spice Islands thus remained in dispute for many years.

Manuel the Fortunate

By the autumn of 1494, when the Treaty of Tordesillas was signed, D. João was a very sick man. The disease which had attacked him soon after the wedding of D. Afonso was gradually crippling him. His hands were now so swollen that he could scarcely sign his name. The doctors diagnosed it as dropsy, but they could not cure him. The death of his son had shaken him cruelly and his hair and beard, which had been a lively chestnut, were already turning white.

The King had no other legitimate children. He had another son, born to Ana de Mendonça shortly before he came to the throne. He was very fond of this boy, whom he first entrusted to his sister, D. Joana, the nun. After her death, he had asked the Queen's leave to bring the young D. Jorge to Court and there he had joined the Duke of Beja in the King's immediate circle. He was said to have been amiable and intelligent, but, though the chroniclers often mention his name, in their pages he is as much a cypher as the Duke himself.

It is understandable that D. João, despite his promises after the Viseu affair, should have wished his own son to succeed him rather than a nephew with whom he had so little in common. But, if this was to come about, D. Jorge must first be declared legitimate. The King needed the support of his family and a dispensation from the Pope. But neither the one nor the other was forthcoming. Although the Queen treated D. Jorge kindly, she saw no reason why she should endorse the claims of the King's by-blow at the expense of her own brother; her mother D. Beatriz, and her sister, the widow of the Duke of Bragança, of course entirely agreed with her. From Rome also, the Pope refused the dispensation; the Cardinal Archbishop of Lisbon, in exile since D. João had uncovered his part in the Bragança affair, was at his side to give him suitable advice.

D. João accepted the inevitable. He could see that his young son would have powerful enemies and that the country would be torn apart by a disputed succession. Although he was still under forty, he knew that he was mortally ill and that he now had neither the time nor the strength to overcome all the opposition to his plans. In the summer of 1495 he made his will: he named the Duke of Beja as his heir and commended his son to his care. To his visitors he continued to behave as if there was nothing the matter with him, riding and hunting as he had always done. But he was desperate enough to snatch at reports of miraculous cures brought about by the medicinal springs at Monchique in the Algarve hills. In spite of the doubts of some of his doctors, he determined to spend the winter there. But, as it happened, the weather at Monchique was cold and wet: the mists hung low over the mountains as in winter they so often do; his lodgings in the little town were damp and draughty; the baths did him more harm than good. After a few days he was so ill that he had to be carried down to the castle at Alvor, on the coast near Lagos. There, on 25th October 1495, he died. He was six months past his fortieth birthday.

In after years it was widely believed that D. João had been poisoned. When they came to remove his bones from the cathedral at Silves, where he was originally buried, to the family chapel in the monastery church at Batalha, it was found that his flesh had not perished. This, said some, was a miracle; others that it was a sign of poisoning by arsenic. But there is no direct evidence for this suspicion, nor could there be, for the man who had most to gain from his death was his heir and successor, D. Manuel. It seems most likely, whatever the disease from which he suffered during his last years, that D. João actually died of pneumonia, contracted in the chilly gloom of Monchique.

In his own lifetime, D. João had many enemies among the nobility; he was not even, apparently, very popular among his more humble subjects, for he was an autocrat and a disciplinarian. But after his death, his reputation grew and it was as 'The Perfect Prince' that he came to be remembered. He was, perhaps, the most distinguished of a remarkable family. No authentic portrait of him has survived, but, by tradition, he is the young man kneeling in the foreground of the panel of St. Vincent, illustrated on page 96.

For more than ten years the Duke of Beja had followed his uncle wherever he went, had hastened to do his every bidding and had expressed, as far as one can tell, no single opinion of his own, even when his own future was at risk. But at the last, when D. João sent messages to him from Alvor, each more urgent than the one before, begging him to come to him before he died, he paid no heed. His sister the Queen, he said, had more need of him than a dying King.

D. Manuel, 'The Fortunate', was to become the ruler of the greatest empire the world had so far seen. Not for him the heartbreaks and frustrations against which his predecessors had struggled for almost eighty years. The golden harvest of the Indies fell into his lap almost without an effort. Yet he could have considered himself lucky to have come to the throne at all. It is true that he was of the blood royal, the son of Afonso V's younger brother, but he was born the ninth and youngest child of his family; he had five elder brothers, four of whom had died unmarried while they were still young, and the fifth, the Duke of Viseu, had paid with his life for his intrigues against the Crown. D. João's own son, married and in good health, was killed before he had time to found a family.

In the event D. Manuel's claim to the throne was accepted without question by Council and Cortes alike. The new King was twenty-six years old. He was well-known by sight to many of his people, for he had long been a familiar figure in the retinue of D. João. Damião de Góis tells us that he was tall and well-built, but with arms so long that his outstretched fingers reached below his knees. But no one knew what manner of man he was, nor what kind of ruler he would make.

It soon became apparent that he had a will of his own and that he deeply resented the insignificant role he had been forced to play in the previous reign. Much of what D. João had done he set himself at once to undo. It is true that he respected the dead King's wishes in so far as D. Jorge was concerned: he treated the young man well and afterwards arranged a good marriage for him. But, where D. João had been unassuming and, in the main, thrifty, D. Manuel was ostentatious and extravagant; he was often forgetful of those who served him well, whereas his uncle had always been quick to show his gratitude; he was abrupt and impatient with the Cortes, as D. João had never been. He distributed lands and titles with a lavish hand, recalling to Portugal all those who had conspired against his predecessor; to the heir of the Duke of Bragança, he restored all the family estates, honours and privileges.

This course of action might have been foreseen, for most of the exiles had been associates of his brother, but D. Manuel's next step seems to have taken everybody by surprise. He arranged with Ferdinand and Isabella that he should marry their eldest daughter, the widow of his own cousin Afonso. He was aware, no doubt, that the Infanta Isabella's brother Juan, the heir to the thrones of Castile and Aragon, was an invalid. Like his two predecessors, he was seduced by dreams of a united 'Spain'. But one must suppose also that he was greatly attracted by the Princess herself, but, if this was so, he had, as was his habit, kept his feelings strictly to himself. In any case, he was prepared to sacrifice twenty thousand Jews to obtain his bride. For D. Isabella declared that she could not return to live in a country where unbelievers such as Jews and Moors were allowed to worship unmolested. So, at Easter 1497, the King decreed that all Jewish children under fourteen should be separated from their parents to be brought up in the Christian faith and that all Jews who had not been baptized by October should be expelled from Portugal. In the autumn thousands of Jews who had collected in Lisbon to face a new exile were forcibly baptized. Moors were less harshly treated for fear of reprisals on the Christian merchants and captives in the kingdom of Fez. But D. Manuel was able to report his country 'clean' and marry D. Isabella in the summer of 1498.

One thing D. Manuel did not change – the arrangements for a new expedition to continue the search for a sea-way to the Indies. Towards the end of his life, D. João had ordered trees to be selected from the royal forests so that two new ships could be built. He had put Bartolemeu Dias in charge of the work. Now it remained for his successor to decide whether he should proceed with the enterprise. He summoned his Council to advise him. The majority were against the project. They pointed out that the risks would be incalculable and the cost immense; even if the expedition reached its goal, they could think of no possible advantages which could outweigh the dangers of navigating in such remote waters; the loss of men and money in establishing themselves in lands so far off might be so great that the realm would be greatly enfeebled thereby. Moreover, they must take into account the jealousies which would be aroused in other countries if they were successful in laying their hands on the wealth of the Indies; they must remember that even the discovery of the unproductive Antilles had almost caused a breach between Portugal and Castile; the Sultan of Egypt would certainly not take kindly to a rival in eastern waters, nor the Venetians to a competitor in the spice trade.

But these prudent counsels did not prevail, for they did not accord with the intentions of the King. 'I have', he said, 'inherited from my predecessors a sacred mission. Both my great-uncle, D. Henrique, and my father, D. Fernão, devoted their lives to the cause of exploration overseas and their labours must not be brought to naught. For my own part, I am prepared to leave these matters in the hands of God, in the conviction that He, of His great goodness, will find a way to bring profit to the kingdom.'

D. Manuel chose Vasco da Gama to lead the enterprise. The reasons for his choice are not altogether clear. Gama was still a comparatively young man: he was certainly under forty and may have been several years younger. His family owned land in the neighbourhood of the little Atlantic port of Sines, but they were not in any way distinguished. Vasco himself had been brought up among the fishermen of his birthplace, but he had later moved to

Évora with his father to complete his education. As it turned out, he proved himself well able to hold his own with professional seamen and pilots, but he had not been trained for the sea, nor, for that matter, for diplomacy, which was to be as important a part of his commission as navigation. One account suggests that one day the King caught sight of Vasco da Gama at Court and was suddenly inspired to offer him the appointment. But Barros says that the captaincy was his by right, for it had been offered to his father, Estevão da Gama, in the previous reign[2]. As Estevão da Gama had since died and his elder son Paolo had pleaded ill health, Vasco had inherited their responsibilities.

There were four ships in the little fleet: two of them, the *São Gabriel* and the *São Rafael*, were those which had been specially built by a picked team with Bartolemeu Dias in charge of them. They were stouter but less handy than the caravels on which the Portuguese had relied so far. They were square-rigged on fore and main masts, but retained the lateen rig for the mizzen. No exact measurements have been recorded, but if, as seems likely, they were much the same size as the *Santa Maria* of Columbus, they would have been about 125 feet long with a capacity of about 120 tons. The *S. Gabriel* was the flagship: it was commanded by Vasco da Gama himself with Pêro de Alenquer, who had sailed with Dias, as his pilot. The captain of the *S. Rafael* was Vasco's elder brother Paolo and his pilot was João de Coimbra. The third ship was smaller, a caravel: its real name was the *S. Miguel*, but it was usually known as the *Berrio* after its previous owner. Nicolau Coelho was in command and his pilot was the very experienced Pêro de Escobar who had already taken part in several expeditions, including the second voyage of Diogo Cão. The tally was completed by a large store-ship, due to be broken up as soon as its contents had been transferred to the other vessels; it was put in charge of Gonçalo Nunes who was a member of the Gama household.

The crews of all four ships together totalled no more than a hundred and seventy men. They included secretaries, such as Álvaro Velho on the *S. Rafael* whose diary is the only first-hand account of the voyage to have survived; interpreters such as João Martins, who could speak Hebrew and Arabic, and Martim Afonso, who had lived for some years in the Congo, and *degredados*, convicts who had been offered their freedom in exchange for a promise that they would undertake any tasks, however dangerous, that might be assigned to them. But it does not seem to have been easy to recruit even this small number. In the fourteen-nineties the Southern Ocean had as evil a reputation among the sailors who thronged the taverns of Lisbon's waterfront as had the seas beyond Cabo Branco seventy years before. The King was forced to raise the wages offered from five to seven *cruzados* a month; in addition, every bachelor among the crews was given a bonus of forty *cruzados* to buy what he needed for the voyage; every married man received a hundred *cruzados* so that he could provide for his family while he was away. Vasco da Gama and his brother were each granted two thousand *cruzados* towards the cost of stores, equipment and merchandise.

The stores, the unappetizing biscuits and salt-tack, raisins and dried beans of the fifteenth-century sailor, were mostly loaded into the store-ship and were intended to last for three years. The equipment included the most up-to-date instruments and nautical tables, but even so it was still only possible for the pilots to calculate longitude by dead reckoning and even latitude could not be accurately determined from the deck of a rolling ship. The vessels were armed with bombards, rudimentary bronze cannon which were the forerunners of the guns which for two hundred and fifty years were to be one of the chief props of European power in the Far East. Over the trade goods, the King and his advisers made a serious mistake. They were used to dealing with the poverty-stricken and unsophisticated chiefs and peoples of tropical Africa who were delighted with the trumpery oddments with which the caravels were filled, the copper rings, the barbers' basins, hawksbells and red berets. But the merchants of the wealthy kingdoms of India sneered at such trash and the rulers and notables laughed in Gama's face when he presented the gifts he had brought with him in the name of his royal master, the King of Portugal.

The day of departure approached. The fleet was anchored in readiness off Restelo and the King summoned his captains to the Castle of São Jorge to give them their final instructions. 'The principle aim which I have in mind', D. Manuel said in the course of a long speech, 'after the desire to rule my people in peace and justice, is to increase the wealth and renown of this my kingdom, so that I may reward more generously all those who have served me. No other enterprise will bring more profit to my realm than the discovery of a new way to India and the countries which lie near to it[3].'

Then Vasco da Gama, kneeling before his sovereign, received from his hands a banner embroidered with the red cross of the Order of Christ. 'I, Vasco da Gama,' he said, 'obedient to thy orders, my Lord, most high and mighty King, go now to discover the lands and seas of the Orient. I swear by that sign of the Cross which I hold in my hand that I will keep this banner always aloft before Moors or Gentiles or whatever people I may meet. And I swear that through all the perils of water, fire or steel, I will defend that Cross unto death. And I further swear that throughout that enterprise with which thou hast charged me I will serve thee with loyalty, vigilance, courage and faith, respecting thy orders and obedient to thy commands.'

In addition to these verbal exhortations, Gama received written instructions. Among them were letters to Prester John, to the King of Calicut and to other rulers through whose waters his way might pass. When he had taken leave of his King, he withdrew to spend the night at the chapel at Restelo which D. Henrique had built for the solace of mariners on the eve of their departure. Whatever may have been the Captain-General's own feelings about the adventure on which he was about to embark, there was little doubt among the people of Lisbon, and especially among the friends and relatives of members of the crews, that he and his companions were going to their deaths and that neither man nor ship would ever be seen again. In the *Lusiadas*, the great national epic which tells the story of this memorable voyage, Camões paints the scene on the Lisbon waterfront on that July morning of 1497[4].

> At dawn, upon the long-awaited day,
> Lisbon awakes: from all its quarters pour
> Parents and friends to speed us on our way:
> Mothers and wives and sweethearts crowd the shore:
> (Others, mere onlookers, to watch the play
> And prophesy what dangers lie in store).
>   Sadly they see us pass, their growing fears
>   Marking their faces with their coursing tears.
>
> And we, who spent the wakeful night in prayer,
> In Henry's chapel near Restelo's strand,
> March to the water's edge. The genial air
> Echoes the chanting of a pious band
> Of priests who sing in unison, and there
> Our boats await us: timely from the land
>   The last scant, friendly thread that binds us parts
>   Amid the turmoil of our doubting hearts.

Forlorn, their voices rise in sad lament;
Weeping, a mother cries, 'Now I have none
To be the refuge and the sweet content
Of my advancing years: come back, my son.'
Nearby, bare-headed, with her clothing rent,
A woman calls her husband: 'Thou hast done
  What cannot be forgiven, for thy life
  Belongs not to thee, but to thy lonely wife.'

Amid the jostling crowd at Tagus' side
A sturdy townsman lifts his wise old head,
His deep voice rings across the impatient tide,
Crying his stern complaint in accents dread.
'Vain hope, false promise of your soaring pride,
No glory waits beside the path you tread:
  Hungry ambition and the lust for power
  Reap but the empty plaudits of an hour.'

'What men call fame is often dearly bought
With dangerous tempests, thoughtless cruelty,
Yea, even death: souls to perdition brought,
Loved ones abandoned in impiety,
Estates consumed, proud kingdoms come to naught,
And empires buried in calamity.
  The lure of glory in which fools believe
  Is but a myth which flatters to deceive.'

'What new disasters shall this word conceal?
What perils to this realm and people bring?
What promises of wealth? What false appeal
Of victories, conquests, triumphs, everything?
Unhappy race, whose ancestors dids't steal
The fire from heaven to make the anvils ring
  With instruments of war! Trapped in this iron cage
  Who can remember now the Golden Age?'

'If wars must be, Mohammed's cursed creed
Offers a Christian battles and to spare
Close here at home. If riches be thy need,
Are there not countless Muslim cities where

Lies wealth immeasurable? And if thy greed
For land and honour drives thee, then I swear
   There is than Moorish land no better prize,
   No braver enemy in wordly eyes.'

'The enemy is strong without the gate:
While you embark to seek another foe
In far-off lands, your kinsmen here must wait:
Who knows what perils they must undergo,
Bereft of men and wealth? I see grim fate
Deal this enfeebled realm a mortal blow.
   Uncertain fortune beckons in your dreams;
   Before your eyes the wealth of India gleams.'

Thus the old man our star-crossed fate bewails:
But, as he speaks, throughout the fleet the crew
Bend strictly to their tasks and hoist the sails.
Now from the shore they wave their last adieux,
Now is the time when resolution fails
And grief at parting blinds our eyes anew.
   Yet, ere the day gives place to shades of night
   The hills and bays of home are lost to sight.

The Sea Way to India

On the afternoon on 1st March 1498 the ships of Vasco da Gama, with the red cross of the Order of Christ emblazoned on their sails, appeared off Moçambique and a new era in the history of the Indian Ocean had begun. They had already been at sea for almost eight months.

They had left Lisbon on 8th July 1497. As far as the Cape Verde Islands they had made good time, although the vessels had temporarily lost touch with one another in a thick mist to the south of the Canaries. At Santiago, the largest of the group, they had stayed a week to take in meat, water and firewood. On 8th August they set sail once more and this was their last sight of land for exactly two months.

This period, one of the most interesting and important of the whole voyage, is dismissed by Álvaro Velho[1] in a single short paragraph. He reports that after leaving the Cape Verdes they first headed east; that some days later the main-yard of the *S. Gabriel* broke and they had to heave to for two days and a night while repairs were carried out; that towards the end of the month, while sailing south by west, they saw a flight of herons and, on the same day, a whale.

The course they set was to be followed by ships' captains until the end of the days of sail. For the first part of their voyage they were accompanied by Bartolemeu Dias, recently appointed Captain of the fortress of S. Jorge da Mina in reward for past services. He left them off Sierra Leone

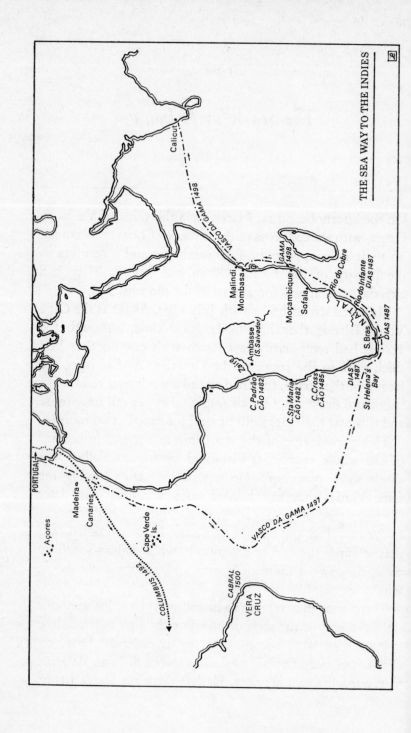

THE SEA WAY TO THE INDIES

Açores

PORTUGAL

Madeira

Canaries

Cape Verde Is.

COLUMBUS 1492

CABRAL 1500

VERA CRUZ

VASCO DA GAMA 1497

St Helena's Bay

DIAS 1487

DIAS 1487

C. Cross CÃO 1485

C. Sta Maria CÃO 1482

C. Padrão CÃO 1482

Zaïre

Ambasse (S. Salvador)

S. Bras

DIAS 1487

Rio do Cobre

Riode Infante DIAS 1487

NATAL

Sofala

Moçambique

GAMA 1498

Malindi

Mombasa

VASCO DA GAMA 1498

Calicut

and it was then, presumably, that they headed south by west. But we can only guess why they had first sailed east from Santiago, towards the coast of Africa. It may have been to keep company with Dias for as long as they could, but it seems at least possible that it was to give themselves sea room when they crossed the Equator. But this suggestion only makes sense if one assumes that the Portuguese knew of land below the Equator to the west of them[2].

With the favourable westerlies at their back, they made their landfall at nine o'clock in the morning of Saturday, 4th November. Velho gives no details of the distance run or of their estimated position at any intermediate point during the voyage. It would be interesting to know if this was a landsman's ignorance or if such information was deliberately suppressed. To celebrate their first sight of land they put on their best clothes, ran up flags to the mast-head and saluted their captain with salvoes of artillery. But, because the coast seemed inhospitable and they did not recognize it, they stood out to sea again for three days until the following Tuesday, when they found a sheltered bay with deep, clear water in which they thankfully dropped anchor. They called it St. Helena's Bay, the name it retains to this day. Pêro de Alenquer thought that they were about thirty leagues north of the Cape and he proved to be right within a few miles.

The Portuguese spent eight days in St. Helena's Bay, cleaning the ships, mending the sails and taking on board firewood and fresh water. During this time they made their first acquaintance with the Hottentots. These small, dusky men, Velho reported, lived on roots, honey and the flesh of seals, whales and gazelles. They wore skins and sheaths round their middles and were armed with spears tipped with horn hardened in the fire. They did not seem to recognize any of the samples which Gama showed them of gold, seed-pearls and various kinds of spices. But they willingly exchanged their few, poor possessions, their fly-whisks and ornaments of sea shells for little bells, metal rings and especially for small copper coins.

Before the Portuguese left the Bay an incident occurred which might have had serious consequences. None of them could understand a word of what the Hottentots said and they had to communicate with them entirely by signs. But, as they seemed so harmless and friendly, Fernão Veloso, at his own request, was granted permission to go with them to their village and spend the night there. The natives killed a seal to entertain their guest, but after supper Veloso suddenly changed his mind and returned to the shore, shouting to attract the attention of his companions on the ships. Góis says that he was revolted by the table manners of his hosts, but, according to Velho's account, the Hottentots themselves indicated that they did not wish him to remain with them any longer. Whatever the reason, the natives followed Veloso through the bush and, when the Portuguese came to collect him, greeted the boats with a shower of spears. Gama and three of his men were slightly wounded. No doubt this mishap was due to a misunderstanding, but it showed how easily such mistakes could arise and mutual ignorance and distrust lead to bloodshed.

The fleet set sail again on Thursday, 16th November, and sighted the Cape two days later. The winds were against them and it was almost a week before they could work their way round it. But thereafter they made better progress, until, on 25th November, they anchored in the Bay of São Bras, where Dias had made his first landfall. Here they broke up the store-ship and transferred what she had in her to the other three vessels.

They spent thirteen days at São Bras without incident. The Hottentots gathered in considerable numbers, eagerly offering ivory bracelets in return for the usual trifles and singing and dancing to entertain their visitors and themselves. Before they left, the Portuguese erected a cross and a pillar on the headland overlooking the bay. But the Hottentots demolished them before they were even out of sight. No doubt they feared lest these mysterious emblems betokened some dangerous and powerful witchcraft, for they could not have felt much confidence in these unfriendly strangers who had appeared so suddenly in their midst.

By Christmas Day the three ships were well beyond the furthest point reached by Dias. They gave the name of Natal to the attractive coast they were then passing. According to Velho, they had for a short time lost the *Berrio* in a storm and found great difficulty in overcoming the north-easterly flow of the Agulhas current. But morale seems to have been reasonably high and there is no mention in any other narrative of the threatened mutiny so graphically described by Gaspar de Correa[1]. Gama is said by him to have put his pilot, his master and several of the seamen in irons and to have thrown all the navigating instruments overboard. 'I have no need of them now', he is said to have explained, 'for God will show me the way'. The early chapters of Correa's book are readable but unreliable and this story is certainly apocryphal.

By the second week in January the Portuguese had run very short of water. They were now in the neighbourhood of Delagoa Bay and, though they did not put it that way, back in the country of the Bantu. They were made welcome by the local chief, who fed his visitors on porridge made of millet and on chickens 'just like those we have in Portugal'. The people wore ornaments of copper on their arms and legs and in their hair, so they called the place the Rio de Cobre. As yet, of course, they had no pilots with local knowledge and on the next leg of their voyage they stood well out to sea, to avoid the unknown dangers of the coastal waters. They sailed past the port of Sofala, where the gold came down from the interior, past the site of modern Beira and across the mouth of the Zambezi to the dismal coast near Quelimane. Here they found a river where they spent exactly a month, careening the ships and scraping their hulls which had grown foul in the tropical waters. The Africans called this stream Kilimani, 'the river by the hill', and on its bank the Portuguese set up a pillar, which they named S. Rafael, because it had been carried on that ship.

Many of the crew were seriously ill with scurvy: their hands and feet were swollen and their gums were so sore that they could scarcely eat. Yet they themselves called the stream 'The River of Good Omens', because here for the first time they saw signs that they were approaching their journey's end. Although most of the people who lived near by were black and wore loin-cloths, there were among them half-castes who spoke a few words of Arabic and whose appearance suggested Arab blood. Two merchants, dressed in the Moorish style, visited the fleet and one of their servants explained that he had often before seen great ships such as theirs manned by white men.

Five days after leaving the river Kilimani, that is on 1st March, the Portuguese arrived off Moçambique. Of the many ports on the East African coast, Gama visited only three, Moçambique itself, Mombasa and Malindi. He had already passed Sofala; later on, whether by accident or design, he was carried past Kilwa, the most important trading port south of Mombasa, and the flourishing island kingdom of Zanzibar.

There was no doubt about it. At Moçambique they had at last reached the frontiers of the Arab world. There were four ocean-going dhows in the harbour and small lateen-rigged craft came out to meet them. These were the 'sewn' boats, whose planks were joined, not by nails or pegs, but by fibre cords, and it was these boats which were said to have given the legendary city of Rhapta its name. The men of Moçambique, they could see, wore garments of fine linen or cotton, richly worked, and on their heads were 'Moorish' caps, edged with silk and embroidered with gold thread. They were not 'white' Moors from the north, but a ruddy brown, as their descendants are to this day: they were Muslims and spoke Arabic, but this, of course, was not their mother tongue and it would be interesting to know if Swahili was already widely spoken on the east coast of Africa.

From 1505 onwards, when the Portuguese first established themselves permanently in Moçambique, the town was to become the most important port of call on the India run. Vessels, both outward and homeward bound, often had to spend weeks or even months there while they waited for the change in the monsoon and a favourable wind to take them on their way. But both the island where the town lay and the mainland close by were exceedingly unhealthy and many of those who were delayed there died, so that Barros, writing fifty years later, could say, 'There is hardly any place under our rule where more Portuguese lie buried'.

At first the Sultan of Moçambique, whom Góis calls Caçoeija[4], was friendly enough, for he supposed these unexpected strangers to be Turks or Moors from the north and Muslims like himself. He came on board the *S. Gabriel* with a crowd of attendants and was received with as much ceremony as was possible under the circumstances. Those who had no fine clothes and the many invalids were carefully kept out of sight. The Sultan arranged for local merchants to sell Gama all that he needed for his voyage and promised to send him two pilots. Through an interpreter, a sailor who had been imprisoned by the Moors and who spoke Arabic well, Gama learnt that the dhows in the harbour were laden with gold, silver, cloves, pepper and ginger, with silver rings, pearls, rubies and other gems, all widely used in Moçambique and all, save the gold, brought from distant lands, from countries, he was told, where spices and precious stones were so plentiful that there was no need to buy them, for they could be gathered by the basketful.

These friendly relations did not last. In some way or other the Sultan's suspicions were aroused, perhaps by the interest the Portuguese showed in a party of Christian merchants, from India, says Velho, from Abyssinia, according to Barros. These men were delighted to recognize the statue of St. Gabriel which the flagship carried as its figurehead, and there and then offered up prayers of thanksgiving to this familiar saint. The Sultan paid no more visits to the fleet and from then on Gama had no more dealings with him nor with the party of Christian merchants. With difficulty he secured the two pilots he had been promised, paying them thirty *mitkals* of gold apiece and a scarlet cloak, on condition that one of them remained always on board.

On the 10th March, after a landing party had been forced to beat off an attack by a small fleet of canoes, Gama decided that further delay might be dangerous. Although he had only one of his two pilots with him, he weighed anchor in the evening and sailed out of the harbour. On the following morning, which was a Sunday, he disembarked his men to celebrate Mass on a small island which he called S. Jorge. But Caçoeija had not yet seen the last of him. The winds were too light to overcome the strong northerly current and, after four days' hard work, they found that, far from making headway, they were five leagues to the south of Moçambique. They put in once more to the barren island of S. Jorge, but, not knowing how long they must wait for a favourable wind, nor what the future might hold in store for them, they decided they must fill their water casks again. Their first attempt was unsuccessful: their pilot, who was their guide, either could not, or would not, lead them to the watering-place in the darkness. The next night they found the wells defended by a small force armed with spears, but they were soon able to drive them off and take what water they needed. On the third night, hearing that a stockade had been built at the watering-place, they fixed bombards on the bows of their boats and destroyed the stockade and parts of the town as a gesture of defiance.

At last, on 29th March, the wind, though still light, was strong enough to carry them on their way. They had spent four frustrating weeks in the neighbourhood of Moçambique and had, unfortunately, sown the seeds of mutual distrust and religious intolerance which were to plague their future relationships with most of the coastal peoples of East Africa. It was soon to become clear that they could trade only from strength and pay prolonged calls only at ports where they had a permanent garrison and a well-fortified citadel. It is easy to blame the Portuguese, especially for such incidents as the unnecessary night attack on the wells and town of Moçambique, but it must be remembered that the 'Moors' were their traditional enemies and that they were a long way from home, with no possible means of defence except their ships and the arms they carried with them. For their part, the Arabs seem very soon to have realized, not only that their visitors were Christian infidels, but also that they had every intention of trying to deprive them of a large share of the trade of the Indian Ocean where their dhows had so long held a monopoly.

On 4th April the Portuguese sailed past Kilwa, which, so their pilot told them, was inhabited by Christians. They spent the whole day trying to beat up to the town against the wind, but without success, so that in the evening they bore away once more to the northward. Somewhere near the modern town of Dar-es-Salaam the *S. Rafael* ran aground. This incident would hardly be worth mentioning, for the ship was safely refloated on the following high tide, had it not been that, while she lay on the shoal, she was visited by some traders with a boatload of oranges. 'It pleased God in His mercy', Velho was able to write a few days later, 'that on arriving at Mombasa all those who were sick [with the scurvy] recovered their health, for the air of this place is very good.'

The Portuguese reached Mombasa on the afternoon of 7th April, the day before Palm Sunday. Mombasa is an island only in name, for at low tide it is separated from the mainland by nothing more than a short stretch of mud. It is hidden away behind a scythe-shaped peninsula, so that even the old town and port, which lie at the north end of the island, are invisible until the last moment to vessels approaching from the south. But it seemed that they were expected: ships in the harbour were decked with flags and, as soon as they dropped anchor off the point, a small dhow, filled with armed men, came out to meet them. Gama would only allow four or five of the most important of his visitors on board and those without their arms. 'It seems', says Velho, 'that the purpose of this visit was to see if they might not be able to capture one or other of our vessels.'

Palm Sunday was spent in an exchange of courtesies. The Sultan sent a present of sheep, oranges and lemons, and sugar-cane. In return, Gama offered a necklace of coral, an insignificant gift which cannot have greatly impressed its recipient. Two convicts were dispatched to pay their respects to the Sultan on the Captain-General's behalf; they were graciously received and sent on a tour of the town. They visited the house of two merchants who were said to be Christians and brought back samples of spices which the Sultan had given them. There was no need, they had been told, to risk the dangers ahead. If they would only come into the harbour, he could supply them with all the spices they wanted.

The Portuguese looked forward to celebrating Mass with their fellow-Christians on the island, for they had been told that there was a large Christian community there who lived in a separate quarter of the town under their own Governor. The next morning, therefore, they prepared to enter the harbour, but, most fortunately as it turned out, the flagship ran aground on the edge of the winding deep-water channel. All three ships immediately let go their anchors. Various Arabs who were on board, including the pilot from Moçambique, 'supposing from this unexpected incident that their intended treachery had been discovered', jumped overboard and swam away. By means of boiling oil, applied to two prisoners on the *S. Rafael*, Gama discovered that the Sultan was only waiting for him to enter the harbour before launching an attack on his ships and their crews.

After this, there were no further exchanges with the shore. At night the Portuguese had to keep careful watch as boatloads of Arabs with machetes tried to cut the anchor cables. Although they now had no pilots and the winds were light and variable, on Good Friday they got under way once more and sailed slowly northwards, keeping as close to the reef as they dared, past creeks full of mangrove thickets and long sandy beaches backed by forests. They anchored at nightfall and in the morning set off in pursuit of two passing boats, one of which they eventually managed to capture. It belonged to an elderly Arab merchant who was travelling with his young and pretty wife, a crew of fifteen, a load of trade goods and a quantity of gold and silver. Gama, who badly needed a friend, gave strict orders that neither the merchant nor his belongings should be in any way molested. He learnt that they were now close to the town of Malindi and indeed, at sunset on the same day, they dropped anchor off the town.

Easter Day passed quietly. To the surprise of the Portuguese, no one visited them from the shore and there were no signs of unusual activity in the harbour. Apparently it was for Gama to make the first move. He consulted his elderly captive, who agreed, in recognition of the friendly treatment he had received, to intercede on his behalf with the Sultan and to explain his great need of a pilot for the last stage of his voyage to India. Accordingly, early next morning, he landed the merchant on a sandbank opposite the town and watched while he was collected by a boat from the shore. Towards evening the old man returned with a present from the Sultan and the welcome news that he would rejoice to make peace with the Portuguese and provide them with pilots or with anything else they needed.

Within a very few years the Portuguese were to ruin the trade of Malindi and impoverish its people. Yet the Sultan remained their most loyal, indeed their only, ally on the coast of East Africa. His original decision seems to have been taken in the hope of securing Gama's help against the people of Mombasa with whom his own subjects were on bad terms and who were their most bitter rivals. But, according to Gaspar Correa, whose account must still be treated with caution, he had consulted a soothsayer who had told him that the Portuguese would become 'masters of all India'⁵, and advised him that he would do well to make peace with them. Such an agreement, he said, would be very profitable to them and would endure for ever.

Whatever may have been the real reasons for the Sultan's friendly attitude, he was certainly intensely curious about his visitors and eager to meet them on that account alone. Gama's problem was to decide whether he could take these overtures at their face value: with recent happenings at Moçambique and Mombasa fresh in his mind, it must have been a difficult decision. However, since it would clearly be foolhardy to set out across the Indian Ocean without a pilot, he decided to risk moving his fleet inshore close to the town, but to refuse the Sultan's invitation to visit his palace, on the grounds that the King of Portugal had forbidden both his brother and himself to set foot on land before they reached India. Meanwhile, he sent off a present, the usual collection of cheap junk such as barbers' basins and falconers' bells which must have perplexed the Sultan very much.

In the end it was arranged that the two leaders should meet in small boats moored close to the shore. Huge crowds gathered by the water's edge as the Sultan made his way to the meeting-place, He was accompanied by his string band and by his royal trumpeters, bearing six-foot ivory trumpets. He was dressed in a robe of crimson damask, trimmed with green satin; a rich jewel sparkled in his turban. His throne was of copper with a crimson cushion for him to sit on and another beneath his feet. One attendant held over him a crimson umbrella to shade him from the sun; another carried his sword of state, a scimitar in a silver sheath. For his part, Vasco da Gama wore his richest clothes and was rowed by twelve oarsmen also splendidly attired. They carried their weapons concealed beneath their cloaks, for Gama could not be certain that no ambush had been laid for him. His approach was signalled by a flourish of trumpets and a volley from the ships' bombards which so terrified the Arabs that Gama had to give the order to silence them.

Velho tells us that this meeting lasted for several hours through the heat of a tropical day. The Sultan wanted to know every detail of Gama's voyage and of the country from which he came. In the *Lusiadas*, the national saga of Portugal, Camões devotes two out of the ten cantos which make up his poem to these conversations[6]. He makes them the centrepiece of the epic and suggests that Gama and the Sultan met several times over a period of weeks. The *Lusiadas* is similar to the *Aeneid* of Virgil, both in form and intention. It sets out to immortalize the exploits of Vasco da Gama and his men and to glorify the royal house of Portugal and especially D. Manuel, by whose orders the expedition to India had been undertaken. It begins, like the *Aeneid*, in mid-voyage; in the *Aeneid*, Aeneas relates to Queen Dido the story of the fall of Troy and all his adventures before his arrival in Carthage; in the *Lusiadas*, Gama tells the Sultan of Malindi not only the story of his departure from Lisbon and all that had happened to him since, but also the events which led up to his voyage and many of the highlights of the earlier history of Portugal. In both poems, the Gods on Olympus take sides; according to Camões, the dangers and difficulties which the Portuguese had faced were due to the hostility of Juno and of Bacchus, who was the manifestation of the faith of Islam. Fortunately for them, Venus was on the side of Vasco da Gama and the Christians and it was due to her appeals that Jupiter and Neptune agreed to still the tempests which the wrath of Juno had let loose.

Gaspar Correa also tells us that the Portuguese spent some weeks at Malindi, waiting from mid-May to early

July for the season of favourable winds. But the more workaday narrative of Velho, which is followed by most of the chroniclers, states that the fleet dropped anchor off the town on the afternoon of 14th April (Easter Saturday) and left on the 24th of the same month.

At the end of his talks with the Sultan, Gama had released into his hands all the Moorish prisoners he then held and the Sultan had expressed the greatest pleasure at this gesture. But, although the meeting had passed off so well and the two leaders had parted with the warmest expressions of mutual esteem and friendship, Gama was still suspicious and still had no pilot. His doubts were kept alive by the crews of the Indian ships anchored in the harbour, who warned him not to trust the people of Malindi: 'their seeming friendliness', they said, 'comes neither from their heart nor from good will'. The Portuguese believed these Indians to be Christians because, when some of them had visited the *S. Rafael*, they had prostrated themselves before a picture of the Virgin Mary at the foot of the Cross, which hung in Paolo da Gama's cabin. Since these Indians could speak only a smattering of Arabic, this act of reverence was probably due to a misunderstanding and their apparent concern for the safety of the Portuguese may well have had its roots in their long-standing rivalry with the Arabs over the trade of the Indian Ocean.

On the Sunday, after two days' silence, an envoy from the Sultan visited the flagship. Gama, impatient to be off, had him seized and sent a message to the shore to say that he would hold the envoy as a hostage until the promised pilot arrived. On the following morning, to the great relief of the Portuguese, their pilot at last appeared. He was to be generally known to the chroniclers as 'Malema Canaqua', a distortion of his Arabic title which meant 'Master Astrologer'. His real name was Ahmed bin Majid, a Gujerati who was indeed a master of his trade. He was no ordinary pilot but a scholar well-known throughout the Arab world for his knowledge of the sciences of navigation and astronomy. His presence in Malindi at that moment was a great stroke of luck for the expedition and one which even the Gods of Olympus must have found it difficult to arrange.

The Portuguese found their pilot an intelligent and well educated man. They were inclined to believe that he must be a Christian, for surely no Moor could speak with such authority? The Captain-General took to him at once, for they were very much two of a kind. Although, no doubt Gama was supported by his own officers and pilots, their mutual interest in the problems of navigation which faced them is the clearest proof that the Portuguese leader was no mere figurehead, but could hold his own with the professionals. They examined each others' instruments; the Portuguese displayed their astrolabes, including the huge, wooden one which had been specially made from them, so large and so accurate that it could only be properly used on a stable base on dry land. Bin Majid was familiar with the astrolabe, but said that he and the other Arab pilots preferred to use the *balestrilha*, a triangular instrument which was the forerunner of the quadrant. If the description given by Barros is correct, his charts were based on parallels of longitude and latitude and not, as were the European *portulana*, on the compass rose and a web of radiating lines joining prominent landmarks.

Gama was well satisfied with his pilot. He made preparations to leave at once. The finishing touches were put to the pillar which had been set up on a promontory overlooking Malindi. A message of thanks and farewell was sent to the Sultan by one of the *degredados*, who was ordered to stay in the town, so that, if the fleet came to grief, future expeditions could be told of their progress so far. On

Tuesday, 24th April, they set sail on a north-easterly course; for the first two or three days they kept the coast of Africa in sight to the west of them; on the Sunday they saw the Pole Star again for the first time for many months. Velho reports that they made good time with a following wind. In his narrative there is no mention of the violent storm to which Gaspar Correa refers and on which Camões built the story of the final attempt by Juno and her allies to destroy the fleet before it reached its goal[7].

When they left the coast of Africa at last, they sailed for Calicut on the easterly course which Ahmed bin Majid had set. They were out of sight of land for twenty-three days, covering in that time a distance which they estimated at six hundred leagues or more. On the morning of the twenty-fourth day, 18th May 1498, the look-out sighted a range of lofty mountains. As the coastline of western India came up towards them over the horizon, the pilot turned to Vasco da Gama with a smile and said, 'There, Sire, is the land you seek'.

Sources

D. João I was the first King of Portugal to appoint an official historian, and this precedent was followed by his successors. It was customary for this officer to hold also the posts of Keeper of the Royal Library and Chief Archivist (*Guarda-Mór do Arquivo da Torre do Tombo*). He was thus in an excellent position to consult the manuscripts and documents on which his work was based. Several of the contemporary and near-contemporary authors for the period covered by this book were so appointed (see Nos. 1, 2, 5, 8, below).

These royal chroniclers did not, as a rule, go overseas themselves. But there is another group, including several of the authors who wrote in the sixteenth century, who held posts of varying responsibility in the Indies and elsewhere and who based their accounts largely on their own experiences (see Nos. 4, 7, 9, 10).

Two of the authors listed, Cadamosto (No. 3) and Pigafeta (No. 11), were not Portuguese, and their books were originally written in Italian.

It should also be noted that some of these authors were mainly concerned with the history of metropolitan Portugal, and only incidentally with enterprises overseas (Nos. 1, 5, 6, 8, below). The rest, with the exception of Camões, devoted themselves almost entirely to the story of overseas exploration and only referred to events in Portugal itself when they affected the voyages of discovery.

Luis de Camões (No. 10) is in a class by himself, for *The Lusiads* is a heroic epic of the early history of Portugal and of the voyage of Vasco da Gama.

1. *Fernão Lopes* was the first to hold the three appointments

referred to above. He was greatly respected in his own time and is regarded as the father of Portuguese historians. In addition to his *Life of D. João I*, on which all subsequent accounts have necessarily been based, he wrote lives of the earlier Kings, Pedro I and Fernão I, and *A Historia General*, of which only a part has survived.

A Crónica de D. João I was first published in 1644, but earlier MSS. exist of the whole or substantial parts of it. I cannot find that it has ever been translated into English and I have used the edition of the Libraria Civilização (Oporto 1945, 2 vols.).

Lopes held his appointments until the middle of the reign of Afonso V, by which time he was a very old man.

2. *Gomes Eanes de Azurara* was put in charge of the Royal Library in 1452 and succeeded Fernão Lopes as Chief Archivist in 1454. He was closely linked with Afonso V and also, first as a Member and later as Commander of the Order of Christ, with Henry the Navigator. By the time he took up his official duties, he had already completed his *Crónica da Tomada de Ceuta* and this was followed, in 1454, by *A Crónica do Descobrimento de Guiné*. He wrote also the story of the Governors of Ceuta, D. Pedro de Meneses, and his son, D. Duarte, but no complete version of his *Crónica de D. Pedro* has survived.

From internal evidence, Azurara knew many of the explorers personally, and was often present when they set sail and when they returned. However, like D. Henrique, he did not himself take part in any of the expeditions. It is most unfortunate that, by the time he wrote his *Chronicle*, or, at least, by the time he wrote the version which has survived, the Regent D. Pedro was dead and disgraced, so that the part he played in organizing the earlier voyages is entirely omitted.

An English translation of *A Crónica de Ceuta* was published in 1936 by George Allen and Unwin, translated by B. Miall from *The Conquests and Discoveries of Henry the Navigator*, written in French by Virginia de Castro e Almeida. Miall's translation is arranged in seven sections, which do not correspond with the original chapter headings.

A Crónica de Guiné appears in the Proceedings of the Hakluyt Society, Vol. 95 (1896) and Vol. 100 (1898).

3. *Cadamosto* (properly Çá da Mosto) was a Venetian merchant, who, by arrangement with D. Henrique, put money into two expeditions to West Africa and took part in them himself. On his return to Venice, he wrote an account of his own two voyages, and included, as an Appendix, the story of the discovery of Sierra Leone by Pêro de Sintra. His information about this voyage appears to have been given to him by a man who had earlier accompanied him on one of his own expeditions.

An English version of the *Voyages of Cadamosto* appears in the Proceedings of the Hakluyt Society for 1938 (Series II, Vol. 80), but they had previously been included in Vol. II of R. Kerr's *General History and Collection of Voyages and Travels* (Edinburgh 1811).

4. *Duarte Pacheco Pereira* was born about 1450 and took part in the siege of Arzila in 1471. He was employed by D. João II in African waters and, owing to his interest in geography, became one of the King's panel of advisers. He is thought to have accompanied Azumbiya to Mina in 1482, and possibly also to have taken part in the 'official' discovery of Brazil in 1500. There is a hint in Chapter 2 of his book that he may have visited Brazil before its 'official' discovery.

In 1503 Pacheco went to India with Albuquerque, where he commanded the Portuguese contingent during the siege of the fort at Cochim. As a result of this exploit, he became the first hero of the Portuguese Empire in the Indies.

On his return home, Pacheco wrote his book, *Esmeraldo do Situ Orbis*, the first *roteiro*, a sailor's guide to the coasts between Portugal and the Indies and to the coastal peoples and their way of life.

From D. Manuel, Pacheco received congratulations for his exploits in India, and little else. He had to wait till 1520 before he was appointed Governor of the fort at Mina. Even this brought him only trouble; he was accused of peculation and ordered home in irons. Although he was acquitted after an enquiry, he lived in poverty for the rest of his life. He died in 1530.

O Esmeraldo was written between 1505 and 1508, but was first published only in 1892. It was translated into English for the Hakluyt Society in 1937 (Series II, Vol. 79). I have used the version edited by E. de Silva and published in Lisbon in 1905.

5. *Rui de Pina* was appointed to the post of Chief Archivist by Manuel I. In this capacity, and presumably on the instructions of the King, he undertook the task of writing the lives of all the earlier Kings of Portugal. Most of these have not survived, but the chronicles of D. Duarte, D. Afonso V and D. João II are all available in Portuguese.

Pina's near contemporaries, Barros and Góis, did not think much of his work and compared him unfavourably with Resende (see below). He gives very little space to the exploration of Africa: in his life of D. João II, Cão is mentioned only once – in connection with the discovery of the Congo – and Dias not at all. This suggests that the information which D. João was so concerned to keep secret from the rest of the world may still have been kept under the King's hand during the early years of D. Manuel, and only released towards the end of his reign.

Pina died about 1422. His chronicles of D. Duarte and D. Afonso V were published in Lisbon in 1901 but there is a more recent edition of *A Crónica de D. João II*, edited by A. M. Carvalho (Coimbra 1950). This edition contains the full text of the Treaty of Tordesillas.

6. *Garcia de Resende*, born in 1470, was a familiar figure at the Portuguese Court during three reigns. He was a page to D. João II, ambassador and courtier under D. Manuel and Secretary to the Treasury under D. João III.

In writing his *Crónica de D. João II*, Resende drew heavily on Pina's earlier work, much of which he left substantially unaltered. Nevertheless, as might be expected from a well-known poet and musician, he added much picturesque detail, and his book is a great deal more lively than that of his predecessor.

Resende died in 1536.

7. *João de Barros*, born in 1496, was brought up from his earliest years at the court of D. Manuel and educated under the King's eye. He was appointed by him Keeper of the Robes to the Infante D. João (the future D. João III). At the age of twenty Barros wrote a romance of chivalry, called *Clarimondo*, and decided that he would write a history of Portuguese exploits in the Indies.

In 1422 Barros was appointed Captain of the fort at Mina and

Treasurer of the Casa da India. An expedition to take up the Captaincy of Marinhão in Brazil resulted in shipwreck and he never reached his post. From 1432 he was Factor of the Casa da India and was responsible for organizing the fleets which usually left annually for the Indies.

In 1552 he at last produced the first volume of his long-planned work, *Decades da India*; three further volumes appeared during the next eighteen years. But in 1567 he retired both from business and authorship. He died in 1570.

As Decadas is a work of real scholarship, dealing, as it does, not only with the exploits of the Portuguese themselves, but also with the history and customs of the peoples with whom they came in contact. It is perhaps the most valuable single source of all, as well as the most readable. Although widely quoted, both in English and Portuguese, *As Decadas* has never been translated into English and the last complete edition in Portuguese appeared as long ago as 1772. It is not, therefore, an easy book to come by.

8. *Damião de Góis* was appointed Chief Archivist in 1548, during the reign of D. João III. He was a protégé of the Cardinal Infante Henrique, who asked him to write a life of his father, D. Manuel. This work was completed between 1558 and 1567. It is concerned with home affairs as well as with the development of the Portuguese Empire overseas.

Góis was accused of heresy by the Inquisition and only the intervention of his patron saved him from immediate arrest. In 1571, however, he was summoned before the Holy Office and 'questioned' over a period of eighteen months. He was finally released, but only into the care of the Monastery at Batalha, where he died in 1571.

During his lifetime he earned the enmity of the Bragança faction by his unfriendly attitude to their pretensions.

For *A Crónica do Felissimo Rei D. Emanuel*, I have used the edition published in Coimbra in 1926.

9. *Gaspar de Correa* went to India about 1514 as a young man and died in Goa about 1580. His *Lendas da India* is a storehouse of information about the Portuguese Governors of the Indies, most of whom he knew personally. In so far as the earlier voyages are

concerned, of which he had no personal knowledge, his version must be treated with reserve. In many particulars he does not agree with the accepted story of Vasco da Gama's first expedition founded on the account of Álvaro Velho, who actually accompanied Gama.

The passages concerned with the two voyages of Vasco da Gama and his later spell as Governor of the Indies are to be found in the Proceedings of the Hakluyt Society for 1869 (Vol. 42). *As Lendas* was completed about 1561, but it was only published in the middle of the nineteenth century (Lisbon 1858–66). There is a modern edition published in Coimbra in 1924.

10. *Luis de Camões*, soldier and poet, author of the great Portuguese epic, *As Lusiadas*, was born in 1524, probably in Lisbon, of Galician descent. After studying at the University of Coimbra, he came to Court and got into trouble over a woman. He had to go overseas in disgrace, first to Ceuta, and afterwards to India.

Camões left Portugal in 1553 and did not return home for sixteen years. He took part in several expeditions from Goa and distinguished himself as a soldier, but he again found himself in trouble for writing a satire about the behaviour of the nobles on the Governor's Council. He was sent to Macão, where he held a minor official post. In the course of these years he wrote the *Lusiads*. On the way back to Goa, he lost all his possessions in a shipwreck, but managed to save the manuscript of his poem. Eventually his friends paid his debts and his passage home. *As Lusiadas* was immediately popular, but he received no reward for his labours and died in poverty of the plague in 1579.

11. *Philippo Pigafeta* based his *Story of the Kingdom of the Congo and the Countries surrounding it* on the reminiscences of Duarte Lopes, who lived in the Congo from about 1578 to 1587. Lopes was then sent as 'Ambassador' to Portugal and the Pope. Philip II was by this time King of Portugal as well as of Spain, and as he was not greatly interested in the fortunes of the Congo, Lopes went on to Rome, where he related his adventures to Pigafeta during 1588–9, together with all the information he had about the history and geography of the Congo and the customs of its peoples.

Pigafeta never visited the Congo himself, but the details he

Sources

included show a greater knowledge of the geography of west-central Africa than was apparently available to the nineteenth-century explorers, such as Stanley, who finally unravelled the secrets of this part of the world and its complex river system. There are references in his narrative to lakes in central Africa, from which it has been argued that the Great Lakes, Victoria, Tanganyika, and the rest, were known in the Kingdom of the Congo in the sixteenth century. But the distances given are far too short, even if Pigafeta was using the Italian mile of 60 to the degree, rather than the modern mile of 69. It seems most likely that his Lake Aquilunda is the vast marshy area from which flow the Kasasi and various tributaries of the Zambezi (see Chapter 9).

Pigafeta's book was first published in Italian in 1591. It was soon translated into various languages, including the Latin version of 1598 by the brothers de Bry. There is a modern Portuguese translation by Rosa Capêas called *Relação do Reino do Congo e das Terras Circumvizinhas* (Lisbon 1951).

Modern Works

Mário Domingues has written a series of 'popular' studies of the period. They are most useful as a basis for further reading, but do not, unfortunately, contain any detailed references.
See: *A Vida Grandiosa do Condestavel*;
   O Infante D. Henrique, O Homem e a sua Epoca;
   D. João II, O Homem e o Monarca;
   D. Manuel I e a Epopeia dos Descobrimentos.
These books are published by Romano Torres of Lisbon.

Elaine Sanceau has lived in Portugal most of her life and has written a valuable and entertaining series of books which are available in both English and Portuguese. They are not, however, easy to come by, as the English editions were either published in Portugal or in limited wartime editions in England.
See: *Henry the Navigator* (Hutchinson, undated);
   The Perfect Prince (D. João II) (Oporto, 1959);
   Portugal in Search of Prester John (Hutchinson, undated).

Henry the Navigator has caught the fancy of historians for a century or more. There are innumerable books and articles in Portuguese covering every possible aspect of his life. In English the most important works are:

R. H. Major – *The Life of Henry the Navigator* (1868), reprinted by Frank Cass in 1967;

C. R. Beazley – *Henry the Navigator* (Putnams 1895);

V. P. Oliviera Martins – *The Golden Age of Henry the Navigator* (Chapman & Hall, 1914). This well-known author also wrote *Os Filhos de D. João I*.

Finally, the two best-known modern works in English covering the growth of the Portuguese Empire overseas are:

Edgar Prestage – *The Portuguese Pioneers* (1933), republished in 1966 by A. & C. Black;

C. R. Boxer – *The Portuguese Seaborne Empire 1415–1825* (Hutchinson, 1969 and Pelican paperback, 1973).

Notes and References

In order to reduce to a minimum reference numbers in the text, which can be irritating to the general reader, I have listed, chapter by chapter, the most important sources, contemporary and modern, which can be consulted for that chapter. I have only given exact references to specific direct quotations.

Chapter 1

Fernão Lopes – *Cronica de D. João I.*
Mário Domingues – *A Vida Gloriosa do Condestavel.*
P. E. Russell – *The English Intervention in Spain and Portugal in the Time of Edward III and Richard II.*

1. Fernão Lopes, op. cit., Book II, Chap. 95.

Chapter 2

Fernão Lopes – op. cit.
Gomes Eanes de Azurara – *A Crónica da Tomada de Ceuta.*
E. W. Bovill – *The Golden Trade of the Moors.*

1. Fernão Lopes – op. cit.
2. Fernão Lopes – op. cit., Book II, Chap. 97.
3. Camões – *As Lusiadas*, Canto IV, 50.

Chapter 3

Azurara – *Crónica do Descobrimento e Conquista de Guiné.*

J. B. Parry – *The Age of Reconnaissance.*
Mário Domingues – *O Infante D. Henrique.*
J. B. Trend – *The Legacy of Islam.*

1. J. B. Trend – op. cit.
2. Herodotus – *Histories*, Book IV, Chap. 40.
3. Strabo – *Geography*, II, Chaps. 3, 4.
4. Anon – *Periplus of the Erythrean Sea.*
5. Azurara – op. cit., Chap. 7.
6. Herodotus – op. cit., Book IV, 41.
7. Herodotus – op. cit., Book IV, 196.
8. Pliny – *Natural History*, Book V, 1.

Chapter 4

Azurara – *Crónica de Guiné*, Chaps. 9-12.
Rui de Pina – *Crónica de El – rei D. Duarte.*
João de Barros – *Decadas* I, 3-5.
Dr. Júlio Gonçalves – *O Infante D. Pedro, as Sete Partidas, e a Génese dos Descobrimentos.*
Mário Domingues – *O Infante D. Henrique.*
Edgar Prestage – *Portuguese Pioneers.*
Elaine Sanceau – *Henry the Navigator.*
Francis M. Rogers – *The Travels of the Infante D. Pedro of Portugal.*

1. The MS. of Morosini is to be found in the Archives of Venice. It has been widely quoted, but see especially Gonçalves, op. cit.
2. *Alguns Documentos do Archivo Nacional da Torre do Tombo*, pp.3–4. This valuable collection of documents from the Portuguese National Archives was edited by Jaime, Duke of Braganza and published in Lisbon in 1892.
3. Peter Quennell – *Shakespeare*, p. 198.
4. *Alguns Documentos* – p. 5.

Chapter 5

Azurara – *Crónica de Guiné* – Chap. 13 et seq.
Rui de Pina – *Crónica de El – rei Afonso V.*

Barros – *Decadas* I, 7-15.
J. B. Parry – op. cit.

1. *Alguns Documentos* – p. 6.
2. *Alguns Documentos* – p. 5.
3. *Alguns Documentos* – p. 14.
4. F. F. Lopes has summed up the modern view of the purpose and siting of the *Vila de Sagres* on pp. 149-54 of his *A Figura e o obra do Infante D. Henrique* (Lisbon 1960). The tradition of a School of Navigation and Geography at Sagres, in the literal sense of the words, now seems to have been abandoned, though only recently.

The details of the geography of the Sagres area are confirmed by my own observations on the spot.

Chapter 6

Rui de Pina – *Crónica de El – rei Afonso V*.
Cadamosto – *Voyages*, Chaps. 1–9.
Duarte Pacheco – *Esmeraldo do Situ Orbis*, Book I, 27–9.

1. Bull of Pope Nicholas V – *Alguns Documentos*, p. 14.
2. Bull of Pope Calixtus III – *Alguns Documentos*, p. 20.
3. This is the conclusion reached by G. R. Crone. See pp. xxxvi–xlii of his *Introduction to the Voyages of Cadamosto* (Hakluyt Society 1938).
4. *Alguns Documentos* – p. 26.
5. *Alguns Documentos* – p. 27.

Chapter 7

Rui de Pina – *Crónica de El – rei Afonso V*.
Barros – *Decadas*, I, Part II.
Duarte Pacheco – *Esmeraldo*.
Cadamosto – *Voyages*: Appendix describing the expedition of Pêro de Sintra.
Garcia de Resende – *Crónica de D. Joao II*.

Mário Domingues – *D. Joao II.*
Elaine Sanceau – *The Perfect Prince.*

1. The voyages which took place between 1460, when Henry the Navigator died, and the end of the reign of Afonso V in 1481, are very poorly documented. It is true that an account of the discovery of Sierra Leone by Pêro de Sintra is included in the Appendix to Cadamosto's *Voyages*, but for the important series of expeditions which took the Portuguese from Sierra Leone eastwards to the Bight of Benin and then southwards again across the Equator, we have to rely on a single chapter of Barros (*Decadas* I, Part II, 2). It must be supposed that the reports of these voyages were kept under the King's hand and were at some time destroyed before other contemporary documents were released to the official archives.
2. *Alguns Documentos* – pp. 26–7.
3. *Alguns Documentos* – p. 31.
4. For the grant of exploration to Fernão Gomes, see *Alguns Documentos* p. 58 (where Gomes is called Fernão Teles), and Barros I; II, 2.
5. The attention which has been given to the Perfect Prince is second only to that which has been lavished on Henry the Navigator. Resende, Domingues and Elaine Sanceau all include the events of 1474 in their lives of D. João II although they took place some years before he came to the throne.
6. *Alguns Documentos* – p. 42.

Chapter 8

Rui de Pina – *Crónica de El – rei D. João II.*
Garcia de Resende – *Crónica de D. João II.*
Barros – op. cit., Book I, Part III.
Pacheco – op. cit.
Mário Domingues – *D. João II.*
E. Sanceau – *The Perfect Prince.*
D. Peres – *Diogo Cão.*

1. Pacheco – op. cit., Book II, 3.
2. Barros – op. cit., Book I; III, 1-2.

3. Barros – op. cit., Book I; III, 3.

The available evidence about the voyage of Diogo Cão has been collated by Peres in his book published in Lisbon in 1957. His conclusions are based on such contemporary records as exist and the evidence of the pillars which Cão set up at various points on the west coast of Africa. I have followed his suggestions.

4. *Alguns Documentos* – pp. 55–6. These documents are dated 1484 and must, therefore, if the suggested dating is correct, refer to the period between Cão's two voyages.

5. For the Soligo map, see G. R. Crone – *Maps and their Makers,* Chap. 6.

6. The voyage of Dias, see Barros, Book I; III, 4.

7. For a discussion of the methods of navigation used by Dias, see J. H. Parry, op. cit., Chaps. 5 and 6.

Chapter 9

Rui de Pina – *Crónica de El – rei D. João II.*
Garcia de Resende – op. cit.
Barros – op. cit.
Philippo Pigafeta – *Relação do Reino do Congo.*
Francisco Álvares – *Verdadeira Informação das Terras do Preste João das Indias.*
Mário Domingues – *D. João II.*
Elaine Sanceau – *The Perfect Prince.*
                              – *Portugal in Search of Prester John.*

1. Barros – op. cit., I; III, 4.
2. Barros – op. cit., I; III, 6–8: Pina – op. cit., 38.
3. Barros – op. cit., I; III, 9.
4. Barros – op. cit., I; III, 9–10: Pina – op. cit., 57–63.
5. Barros – op. cit., I; III, 5.
6. Pina – op. cit., 21.

Chapter 10

Rui de Pina – *Crónica de El – rei D. João II.*
Resende – *Crónica de D. João II.*

Barros – *Decadas* I; III.
G. R. Crone – *Maps and their Makers.*
J. B. Parry – *The Age of Reconnaissance.*
Domingues – *D. João II.*
E. Sanceau – *The Perfect Prince.*

1. Pina – op. cit., 44–8.
2. Crone – op. cit., Chaps. 1, 3, and 6: Parry – op. cit., Chap. 9.
3. See II Esdras, Chaps. 4, 6, 7, but especially Chap. 13, which tells how a party of Israelites, during the captivity in Babylon, escaped eastwards over the Euphrates. 'They took counsel among themselves . . . that they would go forth into a further country . . . There was a great way to go, nearly a year and a half, and that same region is called Arzareth.'
4. *Alguns Documentos* – p. 56.
5. *Alguns Documentos* – p. 58.
6. The letter informing the King of the discovery of Vera Cruz was written by Pêro Vaz de Caminha. It was first published in 1812 and is to be found in *Portuguese Voyages* (Everyman Series, No. 986).
7. The Treaty of Tordesillas is printed in full in Appendix VII of Rui de Pina's *D. João II* (edited by A. M. Carvalho).

Chapter 11

Damião de Góis – *Crónica do Felissimo Rei D. Emanuel.*
Barros – *Decadas.*
Gaspar Correa – *Lendas da India.*
Domingues – *D. Manuel I.*

1. For the last days of D. João II, see Pina – op. cit., Chap. 80.
2. Barros – op. cit., I; IV, 1.
3. Correa – op. cit., I, 7.
4. Camões – *As Lusiadas*, Canto IV, 87–101. This passage forms part of Vasco da Gama's story to the Sultan of Malindi. This English version is my own.

Chapter 12

Barros – *Decadas.*
Correa – *Lendas da India.*
Luis de Camões – *As Lusiadas.*
Damião de Goís – *Crónica do Rei D. Emanuel.*
Domingues – *D. Manuel I.*

1. Álvaro Velho wrote the only extant first-hand account of the voyage. His story ends abruptly at the Rio Grande on the way home. He apparently disembarked there and lived for some years in Guinea. Velho's account was first published in 1838. English translations appear in the Proceedings of the Hakluyt Society for 1898 and in *Portuguese Voyages* (Everyman No. 986 of 1947).
2. For the route followed by Gama and the reasons for it, see Gago Coutinho in the Proceedings of the International Congress of Lisbon (1949).
3. Correa – op. cit., I.
4. Góis – op. cit., I, 37.
5. Correa – op. cit., I, 14.
6. Camões – op. cit., Cantos III, IV, V: Correa – op. cit., I, 14.
7. Camões – op. cit., Canto VI, 70–84.

Bibliography

Alguns Documentos bo Arquivo da Torre do Tombo, collected and edited by Jaime, Duke of Braganza (Lisbon 1892).

ANON: *Periplus of the Erythrean Sea.*

AZURARA, GOMES EANES DE, *Crónica da Tomada de Ceuta,* from *The Conquesta and Discoveries of Henry the Navigator* in French, by Virginia de Castro e Almeida, trans. B. Miall (Allen & Unwin 1936). *Crónica de Descobrimento de Guiné* (1454). Hakluyt Society, Vol. 95 (1896) and Vol. 100 (1898).

BARROS, JOÃO DE, *Decadas de India* (1552–8), Lisbon 1772: modern Portuguese edition, Lisbon 1945.

BEAZLEY, C. R., *Henry the Navigator* – Putnams 1895.

BOVILL, E. W., *The Golden Trade of the Moors* – O.U.P. 1958.

BOXER, C. R., *The Portuguese Seaborne Empire, 1415–1825* – Hutchinson 1969.

CADAMOSTO (ÇÁ DA MOSTO), *Voyages* (*c.* 1465), trans. Hakluyt Society, Series II, Vol. 80 (1938).

CAMÕES, LUIS VAZ DE, *As Lusiadas* – trans. in verse, Sir R. Burton (1870); trans. in prose, William C. Atkinson – Penguin Classics No. 26 (1952).

CASTRO E ALMEIDA, VIRGINIA DE, *Conquests and Discoveries of Henry the Navigator* (in French), trans. by B. Miall – George Allen & Unwin (1936).

CORREA, GASPAR DE, *Lendas da India* (*c.* 1561) – Coimbra 1924.

CRONE, G. R., *Maps and Their Makers* – Hutchinson 1953.

DOMINGUES, MÁRIO, *A Vida do Condestavel* – Romano Torres, Lisbon 1957. *O Infante D. Henrique, O Homen e a Sua Epoca* – Torres 1957. *D. João II, O Homen e O Monarca* – Torres, 1960. *D. Manuel I e a Epopeia dos Descobrimentos* – Torres 1960.

GÓIS, DAMIÃO DE, *Crónica do Felissimo Rei D. Emanuel* (1556–67) – Coimbra 1926.

GONÇALVES, DR. JÚLIO, *O Infante D. Pedro, As Sete Partidas, e A Génese dos Descobrimentos* – (1950).

HERODOTUS, *Histories* (5th century B.C.) trans.: Aubrey de Selincourt – Penguin Classics (1954).

LOPES, F. F., *A Figura e o Obra do Infante D. Henrique* – Lisbon (1960).

LOPES, FERNÃO, *Crónica de D. João I* – Libraria Civilizaçao – Oporto 1945 (2 vols.).

MAJOR, R. H., *The Life of Henry the Navigator* (1868) – repr. Frank Cass (1967).

MARTINS, J. P. OLIVIERA, *The Golden Age of Henry the Navigator* – Chapman & Hall (1914).

PACHECO PEREIRA, DUARTE, *Esmeraldo do Situ Orbis* (*c.* 1508) – Hakluyt Society, Series II, Vol. 79 (1937).

PARRY, J. H., *Age of Reconnaissance* – Weidenfeld & Nicholson (1963).

PERES, D., *Diogo Cão* – Lisbon (1957).

PINA, RUI DE, *Crónica de El–rei D. Duarte* (*c.* 1415) – Lisbon (1901). *Crónica de El–rei D. Afonso V* (*c.* 1416) – Lisbon (1901). *Crónica de El–rei D. João II* (*c.* 1418) – edited by A. M. Carvalho, Coimbra (1950).

PIGAFETA, PHILIPPO, *Relação do Reino do Congo e das Terras Circum-vizinhas* – original in Italian – trans. into Portuguese by Rosa Capēas – Lisbon (1951): trans. into English: Purchas, *His Pilgrimes* – repr. Glasgow (1905).

PLINY THE ELDER, *Natural History* (1st century A.D.) – trans. H. Rackham – Loeb Classical Library 1940–62 (10 vols.).

PRESTAGE, EDGAR, *The Portuguese Pioneers* (1933) – repr. A. & C. Black (1966).

RESENDE, GARCIA DE, *Crónica dos Valiosos e Insegnes Feitos del Rei D. João II* (1545).

ROGERS, FRANCIS M., *The Travels of the Infante D. Pedro of Portugal* – Harvard University Press (1961).

RUSSELL, P. E., *The English Intervention in Spain and Portugal in the Time of Edward III and Richard II* – O.U.P. (1955).

SANCEAU, ELAINE, *Henry the Navigator* – Hutchinson (undated). *The Perfect Prince* – Oporto (1959). *Portugal in Search of Prester John* – Hutchinson (undated).

STRABO, *Geography* (1st century A.D.) – trans. by H. L. Jones – Loeb Classical Library (8 vols. 1919–32).

Bibliography

TREND, J. B., contribution to *The Legacy of Islam,* edited by Sir T. Arnold – O.U.P. (1931).

VAZ, PEDRO, *Carta do Achamento da Terra do Brazil* – trans. by C. Ley – Everyman Series No. 986 (1947). See *As Grandes Viagens Portuguesas* – (Lisbon undated, but modern).

VELHO, ÁLVARO, *Viagem de Vasco da Gama em Descobrimento da India pelo Cabo da Boa Esperança* (1497) – trans. by E. G. Ravenstein – Everyman Series No. 986 (1947). See also *As Grandes Viagens Portuguesas* (Series I) – Lisbon (undated).

Index

Index

Index